# Equal Protection

# Exploring the Constitution Series

## by Darien A. McWhirter

*The Separation of Church and State*
*Freedom of Speech, Press, and Assembly*
*Search, Seizure, and Privacy*
*Equal Protection*

# Equal Protection

by
**Darien A. McWhirter**

*Exploring the Constitution Series*
*Darien A. McWhirter, Series Editor*

**Oryx Press**
1995

*The rare Arabian Oryx is believed to have inspired the myth of the unicorn. This desert antelope became virtually extinct in the early 1960s. At that time several groups of international conservationists arranged to have 9 animals sent to the Phoenix Zoo to be the nucleus of a captive breeding herd. Today the Oryx population is over 800 and nearly 400 have been returned to reserves in the Middle East.*

© 1995 by Darien A. McWhirter
Published by The Oryx Press
4041 North Central at Indian School Road
Phoenix, Arizona 85012-3397

Published simultaneously in Canada
Printed and Bound in the United States of America

∞The paper used in this publication meets the minimum requirements of American National Standard for Information Science—Permanence of Paper for Printed Library Materials, ANSI Z39.48, 1984.

This publication is designed to provide accurate and authoritative information in regard to the subject matter covered. It is sold with the understanding that the publisher is not engaged in rendering legal, accounting, or other professional services. If legal advice or other expert assistance is required, the services of a competent professional should be sought.
*From a Declaration of Principles jointly adopted by a Committee of the American Bar Association and the Committee of Publishers.*

*Library of Congress Cataloging-in-Publication Data*
McWhirter, Darien A. (Darien Auburn)
  Equal protection / by Darien A. McWhirter.
    p.    cm. — (Exploring the Constitution series)
  Includes bibliographical references and index.
  ISBN 0-89774-855-7 (alk. paper)
  1. Equality before the law—United States—Cases. I. Title. II. Series.
KF4764.A7M33    1994
342.73'085—dc20                                                        94-37866
[347.30285]                                                                CIP

# CONTENTS

❋ ❋ ❋ ❋ ❋ ❋ ❋ ❋ ❋

# SERIES STATEMENT

❋ ❋ ❋ ❋ ❋ ❋ ❋ ❋

The Constitution of the United States is one of the most important documents ever written, but it is not just of historical interest. Over two centuries after its adoption, the Constitution continues to influence the lives of everyone in the United States. Many of the most divisive social issues, from abortion to free speech, have been and are being resolved by the U.S. Supreme Court through interpretation of the U.S. Constitution.

Yet much of what has been written about these Supreme Court decisions and the Constitution itself has served only to confuse people who would like to understand exactly what the Court has ruled and exactly what the Constitution means. So much of the discussion revolves around what the Constitution *should* mean that what the Constitution actually *does* mean is obscured.

The Exploring the Constitution Series provides a basic introduction to important areas of constitutional law. While the books in this series are appropriate for a general audience, every effort has been made to ensure that they are especially accessible to high school and college students.

Each volume contains a general introduction to a particular constitutional issue combined with excerpts from significant Supreme Court decisions in that area. The text of the Constitution, a chronological listing of the Supreme Court justices, and a glossary of legal terms are included in each volume. This series strives to provide an objective analysis of the Court's interpretation of constitutional issues with an emphasis on how that interpretation has evolved over time.

# PREFACE

* * * * * * * *

No area of constitutional decision making has generated more social conflict than that of equal protection. From the end of the Civil War to the present, the problem of providing equal protection under the law for everyone, regardless of race, wealth, sex, or place of residence, has been the fundamental problem of American society. This is not a problem that will be solved easily. Rather, it has taken major changes in the thinking of the Supreme Court justices and the political leaders of the United States to make equal protection of the law a reality for many Americans. No other set of Supreme Court decisions has so touched the daily lives of the citizens of the United States as the decisions the Court has handed down in interpreting the Equal Protection Clause of the Fourteenth Amendment.*

## PURPOSE

While this volume is written for everyone, every effort has been made to make the discussion interesting and accessible to high school and college students. Issues and Supreme Court decisions have been chosen with an eye to what students might find interesting. Cases involving schools have been included whenever appropriate.

---

*Editor's Note:* In fact, as this book goes to press, the people in California have voted 59 percent in favor, versus 41 percent opposed, to deny education and most health care to illegal immigrants. The day after this measure (Proposition 187) was passed, it was challenged in federal and state courts, and it is possible that the Supreme Court will have to rule on this case.

This volume is intended to be useful both as a reference work and as a supplement to the standard textbook in social studies, history, government, political science, and law classes. The Supreme Court decisions reprinted here were chosen because of their importance and the likelihood that they would stimulate discussion about the issues presented in this volume. Teachers should consider having students read only the actual Court decisions in preparation for class discussion, and then having students read the discussion material following the class discussion.

In addition to excerpts of the actual texts of some of the most important Supreme Court decisions in this area, this volume provides the reader with discussions that place those decisions into their legal and historical context. While other sources provide either analysis or the text of Supreme Court decisions, this volume attempts to provide both in a format that will stimulate thinking and provide a general overview to this important area of constitutional law. Both the discussion and the decisions are necessary for anyone who is really interested in understanding how the Supreme Court has interpreted the Equal Protection Clause of the Fourteenth Amendment. It is assumed, however, that readers have a general understanding of how the American legal system works and the role of the U.S. Supreme Court in that system.

Other sources have discussed some of the material presented here, but such discussions usually only present one side of the debate. This volume attempts to explain as objectively as possible what the Supreme Court has ruled in this area. Supreme Court decisions are criticized to the extent they do not logically follow from earlier decisions, not because they fail to live up to the personal beliefs of the author concerning what the Court should rule in this complex area of constitutional law.

## ARRANGEMENT

This volume discusses all the major equal protection issues that the Supreme Court has addressed. Chapter 2 examines the Court's decisions about the meaning of equal protection of the law. Chapter 3 discusses the complex area of public school integration in order to fulfill the promise of equal protection. Chapter 4 looks at when governments may use affirmative action plans in order to try to bring about more racial integration. Chapter 5 explores the difficult area of what Congress may do to fulfill the commands of the Thirteenth, Fourteenth, and Fifteenth Amendments. Chapter 6 traces the development of the idea that equal protection also protects against sex discrimination. Chapter 7 examines the right poor people and people who live in cities have to the equal protection of the laws.

Each of the six substantive chapters (2 through 7) is divided into three parts. The first part, "Discussion," provides an overview of the important Supreme Court decisions in a particular area to show the development of the Supreme Court's thinking over time. Each of the substantive chapters also contains excerpts from the text of Supreme Court decisions that illustrate the major issues under discussion and the logic behind the Court's thinking in each area. Discussion questions at the end of each of these chapters are intended to stimulate both thought and discussion.

The table of cases provides references to all of the Supreme Court decisions discussed in the text. Anyone wishing to read the actual decisions may find them by showing the reference to a librarian in a library that contains the Supreme Court's decisions. The citation 374 U.S. 203 (1963), for example, tells us that the decision was made in 1963 and that the text of the decision is contained in volume 374 of the *United States Reports* at page 203.

The glossary is included to provide a ready reference, but readers may wish to research some of the terms further. Not every term found in the glossary will be found in each volume of this series.

This volume contains two appendixes. Appendix A contains the complete text of the Constitution. Appendix B contains a chronological listing of all the justices who have sat on the U.S. Supreme Court.

When the states ratified the Fourteenth Amendment in 1868, the Union army still occupied most of what had been the Confederate States of America. Reconstruction failed to provide the former slaves with the means to become full citizens. Efforts by Congress immediately after the Civil War to bring an end to racial segregation in both the North and the South failed. America would not take up this task again until the second half of the twentieth century. During the decades that followed World War II, the Supreme Court would be called upon to take the lead in making the concept of the equal protection of the laws a reality for millions of Americans. It took great courage for the justices to do just that. It is only by reading the Court's actual decisions and understanding the legal and historical context of those decisions that any citizen can begin to understand what the law is in this area and why it is what it is. It is to that end that this volume was written and it is to the education of those citizens that this volume is dedicated.

Darien A. McWhirter
Austin, Texas
November 1994

# TABLE OF CASES
# CITED IN THE TEXT

❋ ❋ ❋ ❋ ❋ ❋

# Equal Protection

# CHAPTER
## one
* * * * * * * * *

# Introduction

Under the Fourteenth Amendment, no state may "deny to any person within its jurisdiction the equal protection of the laws." With that statement, added to the U.S. Constitution in 1868, the United States began an odyssey into uncharted legal and philosophical waters that is still in progress. It has been a very difficult journey with many detours and dangerous ports of call along the way. Yet it has been a very necessary journey for a nation that began its history with the idea, expressed in the Declaration of Independence, that "all men are created equal."

Unlike in other areas of constitutional interpretation, the Supreme Court has struggled to define *political equality* with little guidance from political philosophers. While the Court could turn to John Locke's writings when discussing religious tolerance or to the ideas of John Stuart Mill when discussing the right of free speech, political philosophers were not helpful when it came time to put the ideal of political equality into practice. That is because, in theory, political equality seems so simple: everyone should be treated equally under the law. In actual practice, this ideal has proven to be anything but simple.

When the Supreme Court justices began to try to enforce the concept of political equality, they found that almost every law treats some people differently from other people. Taxes are higher for the rich than the poor, criminal laws put some people in jail while others go free, and election laws allow only some members of the population to vote. Which of these distinctions are acceptable, and which violate the principle of political equality?

Another difficult issue was slavery. At the time Thomas Jefferson penned the Declaration of Independence, stating that "all men are created equal," he owned slaves. How can all people be equal if some are free and others are slaves? Slavery, along with the racial discrimination that followed, would turn out to be the fundamental equal protection dilemma for the United States of America.

## AMERICA'S UNRESOLVED ISSUES

When the U.S. Constitution was written in 1787, two basic questions were left unresolved: what would be the relative power of the federal government versus the states, and what would the new nation do about slavery? As far as governmental power is concerned, the Constitution simply lists a series of powers granted to the federal government, such as the power to coin money or regulate interstate commerce, and then states that Congress has the power to do everything that is "necessary and proper" to carry out those powers.

As for slavery, the delegates to the Constitutional Convention worked out a compromise. The new Constitution recognized the institution of slavery but allowed only three-fifths of the slaves to be counted when deciding how many representatives to the House of Representatives each state would be apportioned every 10 years after the census (Article I, Section 2). To people reading the Constitution centuries later, this appears to be a very strange compromise; while these slaves would obviously not be allowed to vote, they would partially count when it came time to apportion the relative votes to the states. The practical result of this was to give more voting power to voters in the South in relation to voters in the North.

The Constitution specifically stated that the new national government could not stop the importation of slaves into the United States until 1808 and that this provision could not be changed by amendment (Article I, Section 9, and Article V). Under the Constitution, slave owners could have their slaves returned to them if the slaves escaped (Article IV, Section 2). The second Congress passed fugitive slave laws to enforce this provision, and the Supreme Court upheld these laws as authorized by Article IV of the Constitution.

The Constitution does not use the word "slave." Throughout the document slaves are called "persons held to service or labour." It is important to remember that when the Constitution was written in 1787 there were such "persons" in every state. In the first few decades *after* the Constitutional Convention, the northern states used a variety of methods, such as judicial interpretation of new state constitutions, to eliminate slavery inside their borders. Gradually, the country became divided by the issue of slavery into a free North and a slave South.

There was no Equal Protection Clause in the original Constitution. While the battle cry of the French Revolution was "liberty, equality and fraternity," the American Revolution was fought for democracy and freedom. Providing equal political power to everyone, regardless of race or wealth, was not one of the goals of the American Revolution. The Equal Protection Clause was not added to the Constitution until 1868, when the Fourteenth Amendment was adopted.

Decades after the passage of the Fourteenth Amendment, the Supreme Court became more and more uncomfortable holding the states to the requirement that they provide everyone with the equal protection of the law and not being able to hold the federal government to the same standard. The original Bill of Rights and Constitution had no equal protection clause as such. Finally the Supreme Court, in what some might say was a clear abuse of power, decided that "implied" in the Due Process of Law Clause of the Fifth Amendment was a requirement that people be treated equally. The Court reasoned that people were not receiving their "due process" if they were being treated in an unequal way.

## THE *DRED SCOTT* DECISION

The unresolved issue of slavery became more of a problem with each passing decade as the North developed into an industrial power with free labor while the South's economy remained based on cotton plantations and slave labor. The North became more and more unhappy with the existence of slavery in the South. The American Anti-Slavery Society was founded in the North in 1833, and from then on agitation for the end of slavery became more and more forceful.

The Supreme Court found itself in the middle. To enforce the compromise that had been reached at the Constitutional Convention, the Court ordered that escaped slaves be returned to their owners under the authority of the Constitution and federal fugitive slave laws. After 1808, when Congress outlawed the further importation of slaves into the United States, the Court upheld that provision as well.

The cornerstone of the compromise reached between the North and the South was the Missouri Compromise of 1820, which addressed slavery in the Louisiana Territory. Louisiana was admitted to the United States as a slave state in 1812. Missouri wanted to enter the nation as a slave state a few years later, but then there would have been more slave states than free states in the United States. In 1820 Maine was admitted as a free state, and in 1821 Missouri was admitted as a slave state. This maintained the balance between free and slave states. To settle the question of slavery in what remained of the Louisiana Territory, Congress decided by law that slavery would be prohibited in the Louisiana Territory north of latitude 36°30', which was the main southern boundary of Missouri. Congress intended that additional states carved out of the territory would follow this pattern. Arkansas was admitted as a slave state in 1836.

In 1857, in *Dred Scott v. Sandford*, the Supreme Court declared that the Missouri Compromise was unconstitutional. Dred Scott, a black male slave, had been taken into the part of the Louisiana Territory that the Missouri Compromise declared to be free territory. When he returned to Missouri, Dred Scott sued for his freedom, arguing that because he had been inside free territory he had become free. Although according to British law a slave who entered free territory became free and could not be enslaved again, this principle had never been adopted by the United States, with its fugitive slave laws. The Supreme Court simply could have ruled that the Missouri Compromise was unconstitutional because the Constitution did not give Congress the power to prohibit slavery in the territories. The Court did that, and much more.

It is difficult to follow the *Dred Scott* decision because there were eight different opinions covering over 200 pages, but the opinion of Chief Justice Taney is considered to be the opinion of the Court. Chief Justice Taney not only ruled that the Missouri Compromise was unconstitutional, he went on to rule that black people were inherently inferior and that the federal government and the states did not have the power to alter the status of a former slave and grant him citizenship. In his opinion, Congress did not have the power to grant citizenship to either former slaves or the descendants of former slaves under the Constitution as written.

According to the *Dred Scott* decision, even if the federal government could buy all the slaves, these freed slaves could not be turned into citizens without a constitutional amendment. Of course, passage of such an amendment was impossible as long as half the states were slave states. In a very real sense, the *Dred Scott* decision left the nation with only one way to eliminate slavery: civil war.

## THE CIVIL WAR

When Abraham Lincoln received the nomination of the new Republican Party to run for the Illinois Senate seat held by Stephen A. Douglas in 1858, he stated: "A house divided against itself cannot stand. I believe this government cannot endure permanently half slave and half free." Lincoln won the popular vote in that election, but Democrats won more seats in the Illinois legislature than Republicans. Because senators were at that time selected by the state legislatures, Douglas was returned to the U.S. Senate. During the presidential election of 1860, the Democratic Party broke into two parts, a southern pro-slavery party and a northern anti-slavery party. With the Democratic Party split, Abraham Lincoln was elected president as the Republican candidate.

Eleven southern states then seceded and formed the Confederate States of America. Abraham Lincoln maintained that these states did not have the right to leave the United States. The secession of these states led to the Civil War, which was fought over the question of the relative power of the states and the federal government and ultimately also over the issue of slavery.

On January 1, 1863, President Lincoln signed the Emancipation Proclamation, declaring that all slaves in territory held by the Confederate forces were free. This had two effects. First, as the Union army advanced into the South, it freed slaves, many of whom then joined the Union army as soldiers. Second, by declaring that the Civil War was about slavery as well as states' rights, Lincoln kept England out of the war. England had become dependent upon the importation of cotton from the southern states to keep its great textile mills in production. The South had hoped that England might enter the war as an ally of the Confederacy to protect its cotton supply. England had become a champion in the fight against slavery on the world stage, however, and could not very well intervene in the U.S. Civil War on the side of the slave-owning states once Lincoln declared that abolishing slavery was a major purpose of the war. Of course, as president Lincoln had no power to free anyone. The Supreme Court had made that clear in the *Dred Scott* decision. Whether he had that power, at least over the rebellious states, as commander in chief became a moot question with the passage of the Thirteenth Amendment.

When it became clear that the Union troops still held the high ground on July 3, 1863, in Gettysburg, Pennsylvania, the Civil War entered its final stage. The human toll of that battle was terrible. The battlefield became a giant cemetery as men were buried where they fell. When Abraham Lincoln arrived at Gettysburg on November 19, 1863, to dedicate the cemetery, he began his remarks by saying: "Four score and seven years ago, our fathers brought forth upon this continent a new nation, conceived in liberty, and dedicated to the proposition that all men are created equal." He ended by saying that he hoped the United States of America, dedicated to the principles of democracy, liberty, and political equality, would not "perish from the earth."

## THE THIRTEENTH, FOURTEENTH, AND FIFTEENTH AMENDMENTS

After the end of the Civil War, Congress wanted to amend the Constitution to make it clear for posterity who had won the Civil War and what that victory meant. In 1865 the Thirteenth Amendment was ratified by the states that had not seceded from the Union. It read in part:

> Section 1. Neither slavery nor involuntary servitude, except as a punishment for crime whereof the party shall have been duly convicted, shall exist within the United States, or any place subject to their jurisdiction.

The Republicans who controlled both the Senate and the House then passed laws in an attempt to punish the South and ensure the new rights of the former slaves. Questions arose over whether the Thirteenth Amendment gave Congress the authority to do this.

Because of these doubts, Congress passed the Fourteenth Amendment in 1866. The Republicans in control of Congress did not believe enough northern states would ratify the amendment, so Congress made ratification of the Fourteenth Amendment a requirement for southern states wishing to rejoin the United States. Southern states had to rejoin the United States if they ever hoped to be free of the occupying Union Army. The Fourteenth Amendment was ratified by 1868. It read in part:

> Section 1. All persons born or naturalized in the United States and subject to the jurisdiction thereof, are citizens of the United States and of the State wherein they reside. No State shall make or enforce any law which shall abridge the privileges or immunities of citizens of the United States; nor shall any State deprive any person of life, liberty, or property, without due process of law; nor deny to any person within its jurisdiction the equal protection of the laws.

Because of further doubts concerning the power of Congress to guarantee the right to vote to the former slaves, a Fifteenth Amendment was passed by Congress and sent to the states. Again, those states that had not yet rejoined the Union were required to ratify the amendment as a condition for their reentry into the Union. The Fifteenth Amendment read in part:

> Section 1. The right of citizens of the United States to vote shall not be denied or abridged by the United States or by any State on account of race, color, or previous condition of servitude.

All three of these amendments had a provision stating that Congress had the power to enforce the amendment with "appropriate legislation." After the Civil War, Congress passed a series of civil rights laws and other provisions designed to guarantee civil rights to the former slaves. However, faced with a high national debt caused by the Civil War, Congress was unable to purchase large plantations and divide them up as farms for the former slaves. The former slaves had been told this would happen and many simply waited for the "40 acres and a mule" they had been promised by politicians from the North. Meanwhile, some of the white men in the South formed secret societies such as the Ku Klux Klan to maintain their power in a society turned upside down as far as they were concerned.

## CONSTITUTIONAL DECISION MAKING

The Supreme Court has developed a number of approaches to use in making decisions about constitutional provisions. The justices may use one, or more than one, approach in any one case. First, they may try to figure out what the authors of a particular provision had in mind when they wrote it. This approach was particularly difficult to use in interpreting the Thirteenth, Fourteenth, and Fifteenth Amendments because these amendments were ratified either by a small group of northern states or by former Confederate states as a condition for reentering the United States.

Second, constitutional decision making often involves drawing a line between people or behaviors that are protected by a provision, and people or behaviors that are not. In interpreting the Equal Protection Clause, the Court has tried to draw a line between factors that are relevant and those that are not relevant when discussing equal protection. For example, race was always considered relevant, but sex was not until late in the twentieth century.

Third, the Court may try to balance governmental goals against individual rights, in this case the right to receive the "equal protection of the laws." This is the main approach the Court has taken when interpreting the Equal Protection Clause, but there has been a twist: the Court has engaged in a series of analyses as part of the balancing process.

## RATIONALITY VERSUS STRICT SCRUTINY

During the 1940s the Court developed the modern approach to interpreting the Equal Protection Clause. The major purpose of the Thirteenth, Fourteenth, and Fifteenth Amendments, the Court decided, was to outlaw discrimination based on race. If laws discriminated on the basis of race, the justices would use "strict scrutiny" in evaluating them. This meant that the Court would balance racial discrimination against the reason for the discrimination, and racial discrimination would only be allowed if government had a "compelling reason." For example, during World War II, the Court thought that the need to protect against Japanese attack was a compelling enough reason to discriminate against Japanese Americans living in the western states.

Discrimination not based on race would simply have to meet a "rationality" test. In applying this test the Court asked whether a law was "rational," that is, supported by any "reasonable" goal. The Court decided that almost any nonarbitrary reason would be sufficient.

## EXPANDING EQUAL PROTECTION ANALYSIS

Beginning in the late 1950s, the Court moved away from the strict scrutiny and rationality approaches. Instead, when considering discrimination cases, the Court asked two questions: what is the basis of the discrimination, and what right or activity are the people who are the victims of discrimination being kept from enjoying? This approach is not far from the commonsense approach most people take when they hear that someone has been "discriminated against." Most people ask first: what was the basis of the discrimination? If the answer is race, that is considered to be a major problem. If the answer is the person did not have on a clean shirt, that is not considered to be as much of a problem. Second, most people would ask: how was the person discriminated against? If the answer is that the person has been kept from voting, that is considered serious. If the answer is that the person has been kept from attending a dance at a city community center, that is considered to be less serious. In other words, if someone has been kept from voting because of his or her race, we consider that a serious problem. We are less likely to worry about someone who has been kept from attending a dance at a city community center simply because he was wearing a dirty shirt. In both cases there has been a kind of discrimination at the hands of government, but these two kinds of discrimination are not the same.

From the late 1950s on, the Court developed what could be considered a sliding scale of analysis. The more "suspect" the basis of the discrimination, the "stricter" the analysis and the more "compelling" the reason for the discrimination had to be. Also, as the importance of the "right or privilege" that had been denied increased, the stricter the analysis became. This can be presented graphically in Figure 1.1.

In Figure 1.1, the bases of discrimination listed on the left range from the "most suspect" to the "least suspect." The more "suspect" the basis for discrimination, the stricter the scrutiny of the Court and the more compel-

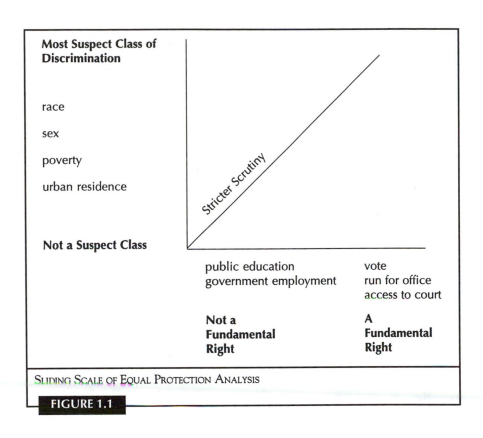

SLIDING SCALE OF EQUAL PROTECTION ANALYSIS

**FIGURE 1.1**

ling the government's reason for discrimination must be. For example, if a government wishes to discriminate on the basis of race, the most suspect class of discrimination, it must have a very compelling reason. If it wants to discriminate on the basis of poverty, however, the reason need not be compelling. If a government wishes to discriminate on some basis other than those listed, such as on the basis of whether or not the person owns a truck, then it only needs a rational justification for the discrimination.

Listed across the bottom of the graph are the "interests" that may be involved. The more "fundamental" the interest, the stricter the scrutiny. On the far right are the most fundamental interests, such as the right to vote, run for public office, or use the courts. In the middle are such interests as getting a public education or a government job. At the far left are the least important interests in the eyes of the Court. If the law concerns nonfundamental interests and the reason for discrimination is not suspect, then government needs only a rational, or nonarbitrary, reason to justify the discrimination. If government wishes to keep someone from voting, government must have a compelling reason.

At times the Court has argued that there are only two types of analysis: strict scrutiny and rationality. At other times the Court has clearly engaged in a "sliding scale" analysis like the one depicted in Figure 1. It is not always easy to decide exactly what the Court is doing in this regard.

## VALUE-BASED DECISION MAKING

Justices of the Supreme Court like to view what they do as the application of legal standards to the facts of a particular case, as if the practice of law is a science. At the same time, social scientists point out that judges, particularly judges who sit on a court such as the U.S. Supreme Court, make decisions based on the values of the society. While the Supreme Court considers social values to some extent in every case, when it comes to making decisions in cases involving the "equal protection of the law," the justices have been very aware of social values, and anyone reading their decisions must understand this. There is no simple "legal standard" to be applied to each case. Rather, the members of the Court read about the discrimination that has occurred in a particular case and determine whether or not this "bothers" them in some fundamental way. If it does, then the law or practice is overturned. If it does not, then the law or practice is upheld.

In making decisions concerned with the equal protection of the laws, many values have played a role. The three values that appear to be the most important are

1. the value of equality in the political process
2. the value of economic opportunity
3. the belief that the sins of the ancestors should not be visited on their descendants

The value of equality in the political process is reflected in the idea that a democracy is legitimate only when everyone is allowed to participate in the democratic process. We see this value reflected in concepts such as the right of free speech and free press. The value of equal economic opportunity, where people are free to make a living, is reflected in writings that have been used to justify the free enterprise system. Many of the Supreme Court's decisions handed down between the Civil War and the Great Depression exalted this value. The value that the sins of the ancestors should not be visited on their descendants is reflected in the provision found in Article III of the Constitution that forbids "Corruption of Blood" or "Forfeiture except during the Life of the Person." These provisions mean that only the person who commits a wrong should be punished, not that person's children or descendants.

"Result-oriented" decision making is the process of first deciding who should win a case and then trying to state a reason to justify that result. Scholars often criticize justices who use this approach. As observers of the Court, however, we must be aware that there is an element of result-oriented decision making in every case, and this is particularly true of equal protection cases. Justices try to avoid this type of decision making because it is very difficult for other judges, who are bound to follow the decisions of the Supreme Court, to apply decisions that have been made in this way to other situations. The less there is a stated "legal standard" for a decision, the less lower court judges can be sure that their decisions on the same subject will not be overturned by the Supreme Court.

As we explore decisions the Supreme Court has made in this area, we will also be examining the different types of analysis the Court has used. The types of analysis have changed over the years, and the type used in any one case will relate in part to the individuals who sat on the Court at the time the case was decided.

## THE SUPREME COURT OVER TIME

Generally people divide the history of the Supreme Court into three major eras: before the Civil War, between the Civil War and the Great Depression, and the modern era. The modern era can be broken up further into the New Deal Court (1941-53), the Warren Court (1953-69), the Burger Court (1969-86), and the Rehnquist Court (1986-present).

### Pre-Civil War to the Great Depression

Before the Civil War the Supreme Court spent no time on the meaning of equal protection. Instead, the Court tried to interpret a Constitution that had been a compromise between pro-slavery and anti-slavery forces.

The Civil War was a great turning point in American history. With the victory of the Union army, the two fundamental questions that had not been answered by the original Constitution—the question of the extent of the federal government's power to control the states and the question of slavery—were well on their way to resolution. After the Civil War, in the partnership between the states and the federal government, the federal government would be the more powerful partner, and slavery would be abolished in the United States.

Between the Civil War and the Great Depression, the Supreme Court was dominated by Republican justices who gave a very limited interpretation to the Thirteenth, Fourteenth, and Fifteenth Amendments, except when these justices used the Fourteenth Amendment to overturn state laws that they thought interfered too much with the free enterprise system.

## The Modern Era

By 1941 eight of the justices were Democrats appointed by President Roosevelt, the New Deal Court. These justices began to expand the protection afforded by the Thirteenth, Fourteenth, and Fifteenth Amendments to individuals, particularly the descendants of slaves.

In 1953 President Eisenhower appointed Earl Warren as chief justice of the Supreme Court, and in 1956 Eisenhower appointed William Brennan associate justice. These two justices turned out to be as concerned about the rights of individuals and minorities as the New Deal Court had been. The period from 1953 to 1969 is known as the Warren era in Supreme Court history, and many difficult issues concerning the meaning of equal protection were decided by the Warren Court.

In 1969 President Nixon appointed Warren Burger as chief justice; Burger was replaced by William Rehnquist in 1986. During this period, through the Burger Court and the Rehnquist Court, the Supreme Court is generally considered to have moved in a more conservative direction. That does not mean that the decisions of the New Deal and Warren Courts were simply overturned—far from it—but the tone and direction of the Court did change. These justices have been less willing to enforce the command that everyone be given the equal protection of the laws without guidance from Congress. At the same time these justices have been limited by the doctrine of *stare decisis*. This is a Latin phrase meaning "the decision must stand." In the American legal system, *stare decisis* means that generally a past decision of the Supreme Court will not be overturned except under exceptional circumstances.

## THE SPECIAL ROLE OF CONGRESS

The Thirteenth, Fourteenth, and Fifteenth Amendments specifically state that Congress shall have power to enforce the amendments by appropriate legislation. In interpreting the Thirteenth, Fourteenth, and Fifteenth Amendments, the Court has been willing to use the stated standards in these amendments to strike down many state laws and practices. At the same time, it has recognized that Congress has the power to go further and outlaw practices that the Court has not been willing or able to control. In dealing with the problem of equal protection, the most difficult area of constitutional decision making, the Court has refused to carry the entire burden alone.

## CONCLUSION

This book discusses a complicated area of constitutional decision making—the right to receive the equal protection of the law. Those of us who approach this issue today have the benefit of both hindsight and over a century of Supreme Court decisions on the subject. We can see what questions and problems have resulted from particular decisions that could not have been anticipated by the justices who made those decisions.

No matter what a person's opinions are about the need to guarantee political equality and the means that are most appropriate to achieve racial equality, it is important to understand what the Court has ruled in this area and why. Disagreement based on ignorance is worthless. Reasoned argument based on understanding and facts is the most powerful weapon anyone can wield in a free society.

# CHAPTER
# two
❋ ❋ ❋ ❋ ❋ ❋ ❋

# Race, Rationality, and the Supreme Court

After the Civil War the Supreme Court found itself in a difficult position. Three amendments had been added to the Constitution through a series of unusual procedures. While the Thirteenth Amendment spoke of ending "slavery" and the Fifteenth Amendment spoke of ending discrimination in voting because of "race, color, or previous condition of servitude," the Fourteenth Amendment was not so limited. It spoke in expansive terms about protecting the "privileges or immunities of citizens," "life, liberty, or property," "the due process of law," and the "equal protection of the laws." What power did the Fourteenth Amendment give to the Supreme Court to overturn laws passed by state legislatures? The Supreme Court began to answer that question in 1873.

## THE *SLAUGHTER-HOUSE CASES*

In 1873 the Court interpreted the Fourteenth Amendment for the first time in the *Slaughter-House Cases*. The *Slaughter-House Cases* combined a series of lawsuits filed to protest an 1869 Louisiana law. The law granted the sole right to own and operate slaughterhouses in New Orleans to one company, the Crescent City Live-stock Landing and Slaughter-House Company. While this company had a monopoly, it was required to allow independent butchers to use the slaughterhouses for a fee set by the statute. The butchers of New Orleans sued. By granting a monopoly to one company, they argued, the law violated the Fourteenth Amendment because it deprived them of their "privileges," namely, the privilege to work free from unreasonable government interference. They also believed that the law violated the Equal Protection Clause because it treated one company differently from all others to the economic detriment of those who were not allowed to own or run a slaughterhouse in New Orleans.

The Court voted five to four in favor of the constitutionality of the Louisiana statute. Justice Miller, in writing the majority opinion, spoke of the history of the Fourteenth Amendment, a history that was "fresh within the memory" of everyone at the time. He ruled that the main purpose of the Fourteenth Amendment was not to control economic regulations such as this one; rather, the fundamental purpose was to protect "Negroes as a class" from discrimination "on account of their race."

Four justices dissented. Justice Bradley argued that the Fourteenth Amendment was certainly intended to protect the "fundamental rights" of all citizens, and that the right to pursue a lawful occupation was fundamental. He also believed that a law favoring one company over all others violated the Equal Protection Clause; he did not agree that the Equal Protection Clause should be seen as outlawing only discrimination based on race.

In his dissenting opinion, Justice Field stated that the Fourteenth Amendment clearly conferred "new privileges and immunities" on all citizens regardless of their race. In his opinion, these privileges and immunities are the "natural and inalienable rights" the founding fathers recognized when they waged war for independence from England, including "the right to pursue a lawful employment in a lawful manner."

The Supreme Court eventually decided that the Fourteenth Amendment did protect certain fundamental rights of all citizens, regardless of race. Between the Civil War and the Great Depression, the Court refused to be specific about what those fundamental rights were, but the Court did protect the right to "pursue a lawful occupation" and other economic rights (accepting the arguments of the dissenting justices in the *Slaughter-House Cases*). In the 1930s the Court decided that the Fourteenth Amendment made most of the Bill of Rights of the U.S. Constitution applicable to state and local governments.

## RACE DISCRIMINATION

Although in the 1873 *Slaughter-House Cases* decision the Court rejected the claim that the Equal Protection Clause protected the right of butchers in New Orleans to work free from government interference, the majority decision did state that the clear goal of the Equal Protection Clause of the

Fourteenth Amendment was to protect the "colored race" from having "onerous disabilities and burdens" placed upon it. Justice Miller talked about the obvious need to protect the "freedom of the slave race" and to secure and protect the freedom of the "newly-made freeman." He also accepted the idea that the Equal Protection Clause would protect other ethnic groups from discrimination, such as the "Mexican" and the "Chinese."

In 1879 the Court, with two dissenters, struck down a West Virginia law that prevented black men from serving on juries (*Strauder v. West Virginia*). Women were not allowed to serve on juries at that time in West Virginia. Taylor Strauder had been convicted of murder by an all-white jury in West Virginia, where black people were not allowed to serve on juries. The Court overturned his conviction. One of the purposes of the Fourteenth Amendment, the justices concluded, was to prevent discriminatory laws such as this one, which clearly denied political equality to black people. Serving on a jury was part of the political process, and black men had to be treated equally with white men. The Fourteenth Amendment guaranteed blacks "political equality," and political equality included the right to serve on a jury.

This West Virginia law clearly discriminated against black people, and the discrimination was explicit in the text of the statute. What if a law appeared to be race neutral but was enforced in a racially discriminatory way? In 1886 the Court addressed this question. In the case of *Yick Wo v. Hopkins*, the Court struck down a law as a violation of the Equal Protection Clause because it was enforced in a discriminatory way. *Yick Wo v. Hopkins* involved a San Francisco ordinance that prohibited the operation of a hand laundry in a wooden building. This ordinance was only enforced against people of Chinese descent. All non-Chinese who applied for an exemption from the ordinance received one, but no one of Chinese descent had received an exemption. A unanimous Court agreed that a law could violate the Equal Protection Clause if it was applied in a racially discriminatory way. The San Francisco ordinance was declared unconstitutional. Chinese in San Francisco would be allowed to operate hand laundries in wooden buildings.

## SEPARATE BUT EQUAL

Between the passage of the Fourteenth Amendment and 1954, however, the Court refused to expand the idea of "political equality" beyond the obvious bounds of serving on juries, running for office, and voting. In 1896, in *Plessy v. Ferguson* (see p. 23), the Court rejected the claim of a black man that a Louisiana law denied him the equal protection of the law. The law required railroads to provide "equal but separate accommodations" for "white and colored" passengers. When Mr. Plessy attempted to use the "whites only" coach, he was arrested. In a seven-to-one decision, the Court refused to overturn the statute (one justice did not take part in the decision). Justice Brown, writing for the majority, ruled that, while "equal protection" meant "political equality," the right to receive equal protection could not be used to force a "commingling of the two races upon terms unsatisfactory to either."

In his opinion, Justice Brown referred to the practice in Boston, both before and after the Civil War, of providing separate public schools for black and white children. Back in 1850, the Massachusetts Supreme Court had held that these "separate but equal" school facilities did not violate the Massachusetts constitution. Justice Brown concluded that the goal of political equality did not prevent states from passing laws that required the separation of the two races in "schools, theaters, and railway carriages" or laws against the "intermarriage of the two races."

Justice Brown went on to reject the idea that "social prejudices may be overcome by legislation" or that the simple act of race separation "stamps the colored race with a badge of inferiority." He concluded that "if the two races are to meet upon terms of social equality, it must be the result of natural affinities, a mutual appreciation of each other's merits, and a voluntary consent of individuals."

Only Justice Harlan dissented from this decision. He argued that the "constitution is color-blind" and that states should not be able to regulate the enjoyment of any right "solely upon the basis of race." He went on to say that, in his opinion, the decision in *Plessy v. Ferguson* would "prove to be quite as pernicious" as the *Dred Scott* decision had been.

The Court's limited view of the power of the Equal Protection Clause is perhaps best exemplified by the 1917 decision in *Buchanan v. Warley*. An ordinance in Louisville, Kentucky, prevented blacks from buying property in predominantly white neighborhoods and whites from buying property in predominantly black neighborhoods. The Court overturned the law not because it violated the Equal Protection Clause, but because it violated the fundamental right everyone enjoyed under the Fourteenth Amendment to buy, use, and dispose of property. The justices believed that the Equal Protection Clause could not be used to overturn the law because, in their view, the law interfered as much with the rights of whites as it interfered with the rights of blacks.

## CREATING STRICT SCRUTINY

During World War II the United States found itself in a struggle for survival on a global scale. The entire nation was mobilized for war, including people of all races. The war with Japan posed a particular problem. There were many recent immigrants from Japan living on the West Coast. President Roosevelt, by executive order as commander in chief, authorized the military to round up people of Japanese descent living in the western states and place them in detention camps until it could be determined whether they posed a threat to national security. In 1944 the Supreme Court was called upon to review this process.

In *Korematsu v. United States* (see p. 29), the Court ruled, with a six-to-three vote, that the president had the power as commander in chief to establish the detention camps. Toyosaburo Korematsu had been arrested without charge and sent to a detention camp for only one reason, because he was Japanese. Justice Black, who wrote the majority opinion, argued that in evaluating a situation such as this, where significant government decisions were being made strictly on the basis of race, strict scrutiny should be applied. He said:

> It should be noted, to begin with, that all legal restrictions which curtail the civil rights of a single racial group are immediately suspect. That is not to say that all such restrictions are unconstitutional. It is to say that courts must subject them to the most rigid scrutiny. Pressing public necessity may sometimes justify the existence of such restrictions; racial antagonism never can.

This statement by Justice Black would form the basis of the "strict scrutiny" analysis the Court would apply in cases of racial discrimination by government. To justify racial discrimination, government would have to have a very good reason, such as "pressing public necessity." In *Korematsu* a majority of the justices accepted the argument that President Roosevelt did have this kind of justification. The protection of the war effort against Japan justified the detention camp process. Toyosaburo Korematsu would have to remain in a detention camp until processed and released.

Justices Roberts, Murphy, and Jackson dissented, and each wrote a dissenting opinion. Justice Murphy thought that without a declaration of martial law the commander in chief did not have the power to establish the detention camps, and that this action went over the brink into the "ugly abyss of racism." Justice Jackson thought that the action was similar to a law that worked "corruption of blood" and punished children for the sins of their ancestors, which was specifically forbidden by the Constitution.

## RATIONALITY AND EQUAL PROTECTION

In the 1873 *Slaughter-House Cases*, a majority of justices rejected the idea that the Equal Protection Clause affected discrimination other than racial discrimination. Eventually, the Court's view changed. The justices decided that the Fourteenth Amendment required any law that discriminated on the basis of something other than race to be "rational." Proving that most laws are rational has never been difficult.

In 1949, in *Railway Express Agency v. New York*, the New Deal Court discussed the rationality requirement. The Equal Protection Clause required that discriminatory economic regulations be "rational," but the Court would accept almost any reasonable justification for the discrimination. In this case, New York City had passed a traffic regulation prohibiting advertising on vehicles but allowing owners of delivery trucks to advertise the name of their company on their own delivery trucks. In other words, a company could advertise on its own trucks, but it could not sell advertising space on the sides of the trucks to someone else. Railway Express operated about 1,900 trucks in New York City and sold advertising on those trucks. If the justification for the law was that advertisements were distracting to drivers, then Railway Express could not see how one type of advertisement would be any less distracting than another.

In writing the opinion for the unanimous Court, Justice Douglas began by saying that the Court would not examine whether the New York regulation somehow lacked "wisdom." In his view, the Equal Protection Clause of the Fourteenth Amendment required that even an economic regulation had to be rational if it drew a distinction between different groups of people. In this case truck owners could advertise their companies on their own trucks, but other people could not rent the sides of those trucks for advertising purposes. While accepting that this was a kind of unequal treatment, Justice Douglas and the other members of the Court refused to overturn the regulation, saying that New York City might have concluded "that those who advertise their own wares on their trucks do not present the same traffic problem in view of the nature or extent of the advertising which they use." He went on to say that "it would take a degree of omniscience which we lack to say that such is not the case."

Later Courts continued to take this very deferential view. For example, in the 1961 case of *McGowan v. Maryland*, the Court refused to overturn a Maryland law outlawing the sale of certain items on Sunday. The justices did not believe that the law violated the First Amendment's command that church and state be separated. The unanimous Court also disagreed with the

idea that the law violated the Equal Protection Clause because it distinguished between what could and what could not be sold on Sunday. Chief
Justice Warren wrote that "the constitutional safeguard is offended only if
the classification rests on grounds wholly irrelevant to the achievement of
the State's objective." He concluded that the Maryland legislature could
have concluded that the sale of items such as milk, bread, and medicine was
"necessary either for the health of the populace or for the enhancement of
the recreational atmosphere of the day."

## BRINGING AN END TO SEPARATE BUT EQUAL

In 1954, in the case of *Brown v. Board of Education*, the Supreme Court
rejected the concept of "separate but equal" in public schools. The Court did
not overrule *Plessy v. Ferguson*, however; it simply concluded that the concept of "separate but equal" had no place in public education. Then, over the
next few years, in a series of short per curiam opinions that usually simply
cited the *Brown* decision, the Court outlawed separate but equal public
facilities, such as public bathhouses, municipal golf courses, buses, parks,
airport restaurants, and courtroom seating. By the early 1960s the concept of
separate but equal was dead, brought down by the new idea that racial
discrimination by government could only be justified by the most compelling
reasons.

## OVERTURNING INTERRACIAL LAWS

Between the Civil War and World War II the Court upheld laws that
punished a variety of interracial activities, including interracial marriages.
For example, in 1882 a unanimous Court upheld an Alabama law that
imposed more severe penalties for crimes such as adultery and fornication if
the people involved were of different races (*Pace v. Alabama*). The justices
reasoned that these kinds of laws applied to whites and blacks equally because
both people involved received the severe penalties.

In 1967, in the case of *Loving v. Virginia*, the Court finally ruled that laws
against interracial marriage violated the Equal Protection Clause. Richard
Loving, a white man, and Mildred Jeter, a black woman, were married in the
District of Columbia in June 1958. They then returned to their home in
Virginia. A Virginia jury found them guilty of violating Virginia's law against
interracial marriage. The judge sentenced them to one year in prison but
agreed to suspend the sentence if they left Virginia and never came back. The

Lovings moved to the District of Columbia and sued to have their conviction set aside because it violated the Fourteenth Amendment.

Chief Justice Warren, writing for a unanimous Court, ruled that states could no longer outlaw interracial marriage and argued that the prohibition had a negative effect on both races. Clearly, such laws were intended and used to maintain a system of racial segregation. Chief Justice Warren also ruled that this kind of statute violated the newly developed right to privacy because it interfered with each person's right to decide free from unreasonable government interference whom he or she would marry.

## CONCLUSION

Between the Civil War and World War II, the Supreme Court outlawed some kinds of racial discrimination by government but accepted the basic idea of separate but equal. In many states, this idea formed the basis of a legal system that maintained and strengthened racial segregation. In the Court's opinion, "separate but equal" laws did not violate the Equal Protection Clause because "equality" was maintained. The Court rejected the idea that "equality" required integration. During those years, the Court believed that, although people should not be discriminated against because of race, interracial laws, such as laws prohibiting marriages between people of different races, did not violate the Equal Protection Clause because they punished both the black person and the white person equally.

Beginning in 1944, however, the Court began to look at these ideas through the eyes of justices who had witnessed the death of hundreds of thousands of American soldiers of all races to preserve, protect, and defend the Constitution of the United States. Could it be that this Constitution really allowed returning soldiers to be subjected to the kind of racial discrimination that these concepts created? As the years passed, this idea became more and more unacceptable.

Since 1944, the Court has required laws that discriminate on the basis of race to be justified by the most compelling reasons. Only two reasons have been found to be compelling enough. The first, the need to guarantee the survival of the nation in time of war, justified sending Japanese Americans to detention camps during World War II. Since World War II, this reason has never been used again to justify racial discrimination. The second compelling reason is the desire to make up for past intentional discrimination and for current racial prejudice through the use of affirmative action plans. Affirmative action will be discussed further in chapter 4.

When Justice Miller wrote the majority decision in the *Slaughter-House Cases*, the memory of the Civil War was fresh in his mind. After the Civil War the nation tried to create a society in which black and white citizens were treated separately but, supposedly, equally under the law. After World War II the nation took up the difficult challenge of creating real political equality. The challenge is still a difficult one, but one the nation must meet in order to fulfill the promise Abraham Lincoln made at Gettysburg to take from the honored dead an

> increased devotion to that cause for which they . . . gave the last full measure of devotion; . . . that these dead shall not have died in vain; that this nation, under God, shall have a new birth of freedom, and that government of the people, by the people, for the people shall not perish from the earth.

## CASE DECISIONS

The 1896 decision which found the concept of "separate but equal" to be compatible with the Equal Protection Clause was *Plessy v. Ferguson*. The seven-justice majority ruled that a Louisiana law requiring railroads to provide separate but equal passenger cars for members of the "white and colored races" did not violate the Fourteenth Amendment. Justice Brown wrote the opinion for the majority, which is included here. Justice Harlan, the only dissenting justice, wrote a dissenting opinion, which is also included.

The 1944 decision establishing the principle that racial discrimination must be justified by a compelling reason and be subjected to strict scrutiny is *Korematsu v. United States*. Toyosaburo Korematsu was imprisoned for violating military orders requiring all people of Japanese descent in California to report to assembly areas from which they would be transported to detention camps to determine whether they posed a threat to the war effort. Justice Black's opinion for the six-justice majority is included here. Justice Murphy wrote a dissenting opinion, which is also included. Justice Frankfurter wrote a concurring opinion and Justices Roberts and Jackson wrote dissenting opinions; these opinions are not included.

Following are excerpts from the case decisions.

❋ ❋ ❋ ❋ ❋ ❋ ❋ ❋ ❋

## PLESSY v. FERGUSON
### 163 U.S. 537 (1896)

MR. JUSTICE BROWN . . . delivered the opinion of the Court.

This case turns upon the constitutionality of an act of the general assembly of the state of Louisiana, passed in 1890, providing for separate railway carriages for the white and colored races. Acts 1890, No. 111, p. 152.

The first section of the statute enacts "that all railway companies carrying passengers in their coaches in this state, shall provide equal but separate accommodations for the white, and colored races, by providing two or more passenger coaches for each passenger train, or by dividing the passenger coaches by a partition so as to secure separate accommodations: provided, that this section shall not be construed to apply to street railroads. No person or persons shall be permitted to occupy seats in coaches, other than the ones assigned to them, on account of the race they belong to." . . .

The information filed in the criminal district court charged, in substance, that Plessy, being a passenger between two stations within the state of Louisiana, was assigned by officers of the company to the coach used for the race to which he belonged, but he insisted upon going into a coach used by the race to which he did not belong. Neither in the information nor plea was his particular race or color averred.

The petition for the writ of prohibition averred that petitioner was seven-eighths Caucasian and one-eighth African blood; that the mixture of colored blood was not discernible in him; and that he was entitled to every right, privilege, and immunity secured to citizens of the United States of the white race; and that, upon such theory, he took possession of a vacant seat in a coach where passengers of the white race were accommodated, and was ordered by the conductor to vacate said coach, and take a seat in another, assigned to persons of the colored race, and, having refused to comply with such demand, he was forcibly ejected, with the aid of a police officer, and imprisoned in the parish jail to answer a charge of having violated the above act.

The constitutionality of this act is attacked upon the ground that it conflicts both with the thirteenth amendment of the constitution, abolishing slavery, and the fourteenth amendment, which prohibits certain restrictive legislation on the part of the states.

That it does not conflict with the thirteenth amendment, which abolished slavery and involuntary servitude, except as a punishment for crime, is too clear for argument. Slavery implies involuntary servitude,—a state of bondage; the ownership of mankind as a chattel, or, at least, the control of the labor and services of one man for the benefit of another, and the absence of a legal right to the disposal of his own person, property, and services. This amendment was said in the *Slaughter-House Cases*, 16 Wall. 36, to have been intended primarily to abolish slavery, as it had been previously known in this country, and that it equally forbade Mexican peonage or the Chinese coolie trade, when they amounted to slavery or involuntary servitude, and that the use of the word "servitude" was intended to prohibit the use of all forms of involuntary slavery, of whatever class or name. It was intimated, however, in that case, that this amendment was regarded by the statesmen of that day as insufficient to protect the colored race from certain laws which had been enacted in the Southern states, imposing upon the colored race onerous disabilities and burdens, and curtailing their rights in the pursuit of life, liberty, and property to such an extent that their freedom was of little value; and that the fourteenth amendment was devised to meet this exigency.

So, too, in the *Civil Rights Cases*, 109 U.S. 3, it was said that the act of a mere individual, the owner of an inn, a public conveyance or place of amusement, refusing accommodations to colored people, cannot be justly regarded as imposing any badge of slavery or servitude upon the applicant, but only as involving an ordinary civil injury, properly cognizable by the laws of the state, and presumably subject to redress by those laws until the contrary appears. "It would be running the slavery question into the ground," said Mr. Justice Bradley, "to make it apply to every act of discrimination which a person may see fit to make as to the guests he will entertain, or as to the people he will take into his coach or cab or car, or admit to his concert or theater, or deal with in other matters of intercourse or business."

A statute which implies merely a legal distinction between the white and colored races—a distinction which is founded in the color of the two races, and which must always exist so long as white men are distinguished from the other race by color—has no tendency to destroy the legal equality of the two races, or re-establish a state of involuntary servitude. Indeed, we do not understand that the thirteenth amendment is strenuously relied upon by the plaintiff in error in this connection.

By the fourteenth amendment, all persons born or naturalized in the United States, and subject to the jurisdiction thereof, are made citizens of the United States and of the state wherein they reside; and the states are forbidden from making or enforcing any law which shall abridge the privileges or immunities of citizens of the United States, or shall deprive any person of life, liberty, or property without due process of law, or deny to any person within their jurisdiction the equal protection of the laws.

The proper construction of this amendment was first called to the attention of this court in the *Slaughter-House Cases*, 16 Wall. 36, which involved, however, not a question of race, but one of exclusive privileges. The case did not call for any expression of opinion as to the exact rights it was intended to secure to the colored race, but it was said generally that its main purpose was to establish the citizenship of the negro, to give definitions of citizenship of the United States and of the states, and to protect from the hostile legislation of the states the privileges and immunities of citizens of the United States, as distinguished from those of citizens of the states.

The object of the amendment was undoubtedly to enforce the absolute equality of the two races before the law, but, in the nature of things, it could not have been intended to abolish distinctions based upon color, or to enforce social, as distinguished from political, equality, or a commingling of the two races upon terms unsatisfactory to either. Laws permitting, and even requiring, their separation, in places where they are liable to be brought into contact, do not necessarily imply the inferiority of either race to the other, and have been generally, if not universally, recognized as within the competency of the state legislatures in the exercise of their police power. The most common instance of this is connected with the establishment of separate schools for white and colored children, which have been held to be a valid exercise of the legislative power even by courts of states where the political rights of the colored race have been longest and most earnestly enforced.

One of the earliest of these cases is that of *Roberts v. City of Boston*, 5 Cush. 198, in which the supreme judicial court of Massachusetts held that the general school committee of Boston had power to make provision for the instruction of colored children in separate schools established exclusively for them, and to prohibit their attendance upon the other schools. . . .

The distinction between laws interfering with the political equality of the negro and those requiring the separation of the two races in schools, theaters, and railway carriages has been frequently drawn by this court. Thus, in *Strauder v. West Virginia*, 100 U.S. 303, it was held that a law of West Virginia limiting to white male persons 21 years of age, and citizens of the state, the right to sit upon juries, was a discrimination which implied a legal inferiority in civil society, which lessened the security of the right of the colored race, and was a step towards reducing them to a condition of servility. . . .

So far, then, as a conflict with the fourteenth amendment is concerned, the case reduces itself to the question whether the statute of Louisiana is a reasonable regulation, and with respect to this there must necessarily be a large discretion on the part of the legislature. In determining the question of reasonableness, it is at liberty to act with reference to the established usages, customs, and traditions of the people, and with a view to the promotion of their comfort, and the preservation of the public peace and good order. Gauged by this standard, we cannot say that a law which authorizes or even requires the separation of the two races in public conveyances is unreasonable, or more obnoxious to the fourteenth amendment than the acts of congress requiring separate schools for colored children in the District of Columbia, the constitutionality of which does not seem to have been questioned, or the corresponding acts of state legislatures.

We consider the underlying fallacy of the plaintiff's argument to consist in the assumption that the enforced separation of the two races stamps the colored race with a badge of inferiority. If this be so, it is not by reason of anything found in the act, but solely because the colored race chooses to put that construction upon it. The argument necessarily assumes that if, as has been more than once the case, and is not unlikely to be so again, the colored race should become the dominant power in the state legislature, and should enact a law in precisely similar terms, it would thereby relegate the white race to an inferior position. We imagine that the white race, at least, would not acquiesce in this assumption. The argument also assumes that social prejudices may be overcome by legislation, and that equal rights cannot be secured to the negro except by an enforced commingling of the two races. We cannot accept this proposition. If the two races are to meet upon terms of social equality, it must be the result of natural affinities, a mutual appreciation of each other's merits, and a voluntary consent of individuals. . . .

The judgment of the court below is therefore affirmed.

Mr. Justice Brewer did not hear the argument or participate in the decision of this case.

**Dissenting Opinion**   Mr. Justice Harlan dissenting.

By the Louisiana statute the validity of which is here involved, all railway companies (other than street-railroad companies) carrying passengers in that state are required to have separate by equal accommodations for white and colored persons, "by providing two or more passenger coaches for each passenger train, or by dividing the passenger coaches by a partition so as to secure accommodations." Under this statute, no colored person is permitted to occupy a seat in a coach assigned to white persons; nor any white person to occupy a seat in a coach assigned to colored persons. The managers of the railroad are not allowed to exercise any discretion in the premises, but are required to assign each passenger to some coach or compartment set apart for the exclusive use of his race. If a passenger insists upon going into a coach or compartment not set apart for persons of his race, he is subject to be fined, or to be imprisoned in the parish jail. Penalties are prescribed for the refusal or neglect of the officers, directors, conductors, and employés of railroad companies to comply with the provisions of the act.

Only "nurses attending children of the other race" are excepted from the operation of the statute. No exception is made of colored attendants traveling with adults. A white man is not permitted to have his colored servant with him in the same coach, even if his condition of health requires the constant personal assistance of such servant. If a colored maid insists upon riding in the same coach with a white woman whom she has been employed to serve, and who may need her personal attention while traveling, she is subject to be fined or imprisoned for such an exhibition of zeal in the discharge of duty.

While there may be in Louisiana persons of different races who are not citizens of the United States, the words in the act "white and colored races" necessarily include all citizens of the United States of both races residing in that state. So that we have before us a state enactment that compels, under penalties, the separation of the two races in railroad passenger coaches, and makes it a crime for a citizen of either race to enter a coach that has been assigned to citizens of the other race.

Thus, the state regulates the use of a public highway by citizens of the United States solely upon the basis of race.

However apparent the injustice of such legislation may be, we have only to consider whether it is consistent with the constitution of the United States. . . .

In respect of civil rights, common to all citizens, the constitution of the United States does not, I think, permit any public authority to know the race of those entitled to be protected in the enjoyment of such rights. Every true man has pride of race, and under appropriate circumstances, when the rights of others, his equals before the law, are not to be affected, it is his privilege to express such pride and to take such action based upon it as to him seems proper. But I deny that any legislative body or judicial tribunal may have regard to the race of citizens when the civil rights of those citizens are involved. Indeed, such legislation as that here in question is inconsistent not only with that equality of rights which pertains to citizenship, national and state, but with the personal liberty enjoyed by every one within the United States. . . .

It was said in argument that the statute of Louisiana does not discriminate against either race, but prescribes a rule applicable alike to white and colored citizens. But this argument does not meet the difficulty. Every one knows that the statute in question had its origin in the purpose, not so much to exclude white persons from railroad cars occupied by blacks, as to exclude colored people from coaches occupied by or assigned to white persons. Railroad corporations of Louisiana did not make discrimination among whites in the matter of accommodation for travelers. The thing to accomplish was, under the guise of giving equal accommodation for whites and blacks, to compel the latter to keep to themselves while traveling in railroad passenger coaches. No one would be so wanting in candor as to assert the contrary. The fundamental objection, therefore, to the statute, is that it interferes with the personal freedom of citizens. "Personal liberty," it has been well said, "consists in the power of locomotion, of changing situation, or removing one's person to whatsoever places one's own inclination may direct, without imprisonment or restraint, unless by due course of law." 1 Bl. Comm. 134. If a white man and a black man choose to occupy the same public conveyance on a public highway, it is their right to do so; and no government, proceeding alone on grounds of race, can prevent it without infringing the personal liberty of each. . . .

The white race deems itself to be the dominant race in this country. And so it is, in prestige, in achievements, in education, in wealth, and in power. So, I doubt not, it will continue to be for all time, if it remains true to its great heritage, and holds fast to the principles of constitutional liberty. But in view of the constitution, in the eye of the law, there is in this country no superior, dominant, ruling class of citizens. There is no caste here. Our constitution is color-blind, and neither knows nor tolerates classes among citizens. In respect of civil rights, all citizens are equal before the law. The humblest is the peer of the most powerful. The law regards man as man, and takes no account of his surroundings or of his color when his civil rights as guaranteed by the supreme law of the land are involved. It is therefore to be regretted that this high tribunal, the final expositor of the fundamental law of the land, has reached the conclusion that it is competent for a state to regulate the enjoyment by citizens of their civil rights solely upon the basis of race.

In my opinion, the judgment this day rendered will, in time, prove to be quite as pernicious as the decision made by this tribunal in the *Dred Scott Case*. . . .

The arbitrary separation of citizens, on the basis of race, while they are on a public highway, is a badge of servitude wholly inconsistent with the civil freedom and the equality before the law established by the constitution. It cannot be justified upon any legal grounds. . . .

For the reason stated, I am constrained to withhold my assent from the opinion and judgment of the majority.

## KOREMATSU v. UNITED STATES
### 323 U.S. 214 (1944)

MR. JUSTICE BLACK delivered the opinion of the Court.

The petitioner, an American citizen of Japanese descent, was convicted in a federal district court for remaining in San Leandro, California, a "Military Area," contrary to Civilian Exclusion Order No. 34 of the Commanding General of the Western Command, U.S. Army, which directed that after May 9, 1942, all persons of Japanese ancestry should be excluded from that area. No question was raised as to petitioner's loyalty to the United States. The Circuit Court of Appeals affirmed, and the importance of the constitutional question involved caused us to grant certiorari.

It should be noted, to begin with, that all legal restrictions which curtail the civil rights of a single racial group are immediately suspect. That is not to say that all such restrictions are unconstitutional. It is to say that courts must subject them to the most rigid scrutiny. Pressing public necessity may sometimes justify the existence of such restrictions; racial antagonism never can.

In the instant case prosecution of the petitioner was begun by information charging violation of an Act of Congress, of March 21, 1942, 56 Stat. 173, 18 U.S.C.A. § 97a, which provides that ". . . whoever shall enter, remain in, leave, or commit any act in any military area or military zone prescribed, under the authority of an Executive order of the President, by the Secretary of War, or by any military commander designated by the Secretary of War, contrary to the restrictions applicable to any such area or zone or contrary to the order of the Secretary of War or any such military commander, shall, if it appears that he knew or should have known of the existence and extent of the restrictions or order and that his act was in violation thereof, be guilty of a misdemeanor and upon conviction shall be liable to a fine of not to exceed $5,000 or to imprisonment for not more than one year, or both, for each offense."

Exclusion Order No. 34, which the petitioner knowingly and admittedly violated was one of a number of military orders and proclamations, all of which were substantially based upon Executive Order No. 9066, 7 Fed.Reg. 1407. That order, issued after we were at war with Japan, declared that "the successful prosecution of the war requires every possible protection against espionage and against sabotage to national-defense material, national-defense premises, and national-defense utilities. . . ."

One of the series of orders and proclamations, a curfew order, which like the exclusion order here was promulgated pursuant to Executive Order 9066, subjected all persons of Japanese ancestry in prescribed West Coast military areas to remain in their residences from 8 p.m. to 6 a.m. As is the case with the exclusion order here, that prior curfew order was designed as a "protection against espionage and against sabotage." In *Hirabayashi v. United States*, 320 U.S. 81, we sustained a conviction obtained for violation of the curfew order. The *Hirabayashi* conviction and this one thus rest on the same 1942 Congressional Act and the same basic executive and military orders, all of which orders were aimed at the twin dangers of espionage and sabotage.

The 1942 Act was attacked in the *Hirabayashi* case as an unconstitutional delegation of power; it was contended that the curfew order and other orders on which it rested were beyond the war powers of the Congress, the military authorities and of the President, as Commander in Chief of the Army; and finally that to apply the curfew order against none but citizens of Japanese ancestry amounted to a constitutionally prohibited discrimination solely on account of race. To these questions, we gave the serious consideration which their importance justified. We upheld the curfew order as an exercise of the power of the government to take steps necessary to prevent espionage and sabotage in an area threatened by Japanese attack.

In the light of the principles we announced in the *Hirabayashi* case, we are unable to conclude that it was beyond the war power of Congress and the Executive to exclude those of Japanese ancestry from the West Coast war area at the time they did. True, exclusion from the area in which one's home is located is a far greater deprivation than constant confinement to the home from 8 p.m. to 6 a.m. Nothing short of apprehension by the proper military authorities of the gravest imminent danger to the public safety can constitutionally justify either. But exclusion from a threatened area, no less than curfew, has a definite and close relationship to the prevention of espionage and sabotage. The military authorities, charged with the primary responsibility of defending our shores, concluded that curfew provided inadequate protection and ordered exclusion. They did so, as pointed out in our *Hirabayashi* opinion, in accordance with Congressional authority to the military to say who should, and who should not, remain in the threatened areas.

In this case the petitioner challenges the assumptions upon which we rested our conclusions in the *Hirabayashi* case. He also urges that by May

1942, when Order No. 43 was promulgated, all danger of Japanese invasion of the West Coast had disappeared. After careful consideration of these contentions we are compelled to reject them.

Here, as in the *Hirabayashi* case, *supra*, at page 99, ". . . we cannot reject as unfounded the judgment of the military authorities and of Congress that there were disloyal members of that population, whose number and strength could not be precisely and quickly ascertained. We cannot say that the war-making branches of the Government did not have ground for believing that in a critical hour such persons could not readily be isolated and separately dealt with, and constituted a menace to the national defense and safety, which demanded that prompt and adequate measures be taken to guard against it."

Like curfew, exclusion of those of Japanese origin was deemed necessary because of the presence of an unascertained number of disloyal members of the group, most of whom we have no doubt were loyal to this country. It was because we could not reject the finding of the military authorities that it was impossible to bring about an immediate segregation of the disloyal from the loyal that we sustained the validity of the curfew order as applying to the whole group. In the instant case, temporary exclusion of the entire group was rested by the military on the same ground. The judgment that exclusion of the whole group was for the same reason a military imperative answers the contention that the exclusion was in the nature of group punishment based on antagonism to those of Japanese origin. That there were members of the group who retained loyalties to Japan has been confirmed by investigations made subsequent to the exclusion. Approximately five thousand American citizens of Japanese ancestry refused to swear unqualified allegiance to the United States and to renounce allegiance to the Japanese Emperor, and several thousand evacuees requested repatriation to Japan. . . .

It is said that we are dealing here with the case of imprisonment of a citizen in a concentration camp solely because of his ancestry, without evidence or inquiry concerning his loyalty and good disposition towards the United States. Our task would be simple, our duty clear, were this a case involving the imprisonment of a loyal citizen in a concentration camp because of racial prejudice. Regardless of the true nature of the assembly and relocation centers—and we deem it unjustifiable to call them concentration camps with all the ugly connotations that term implies—we are dealing specifically with nothing but an exclusion order. To cast this case into outlines of racial prejudice, without reference to the real military dangers which were presented, merely confuses the issue. Korematsu was not excluded from the

Military Area because of hostility to him or his race. He was excluded because we are at war with the Japanese Empire, because the properly constituted military authorities feared an invasion of our West Coast and felt constrained to take proper security measures, because they decided that the military urgency of the situation demanded that all citizens of Japanese ancestry be segregated from the West Coast temporarily, and finally, because Congress, reposing its confidence in this time of war in our military leaders—as inevitably it must—determined that they should have the power to do just this. There was evidence of disloyalty on the part of some, the military authorities considered that the need for action was great, and time was short. We cannot—by availing ourselves of the calm perspective of hindsight—now say that at the time these actions were unjustified.

Affirmed.

**Dissenting Opinion**   MR. JUSTICE MURPHY, dissenting.

This exclusion of "all persons of Japanese ancestry, both alien and non-alien," from the Pacific Coast area on a plea of military necessity in the absence of martial law ought not to be approved. Such exclusion goes over "the very brink of constitutional power" and falls into the ugly abyss of racism.

In dealing with matters relating to the prosecution and progress of a war, we must accord great respect and consideration to the judgments of the military authorities who are on the scene and who have full knowledge of the military facts. The scope of their discretion must, as a matter of necessity and common sense, be wide. And their judgments ought not to be overruled lightly by those whose training and duties ill-equip them to deal intelligently with matters so vital to the physical security of the nation. . . .

It must be conceded that the military and naval situation in the spring of 1942 was such as to generate a very real fear of invasion of the Pacific Coast, accompanied by fears of sabotage and espionage in that area. The military command was therefore justified in adopting all reasonable means necessary to combat these dangers. In adjudging the military action taken in light of the then apparent dangers, we must not erect too high or too meticulous standards; it is necessary only that the action have some reasonable relation to the removal of the dangers of invasion, sabotage and espionage. But the exclusion, either temporarily or permanently, of all persons with Japanese blood in their veins has no such reasonable relation. And that relation is lacking because the exclusion order necessarily must rely for its reasonableness upon the assumption that *all* persons of Japanese ancestry may have a dangerous tendency to commit sabotage and espionage and to aid our Japanese enemy in other ways. It is difficult to believe that reason, logic or experience could be marshalled in support of such an assumption. . . .

No adequate reason is given for the failure to treat these Japanese Americans on an individual basis by holding investigations and hearings to separate the loyal from the disloyal, as was done in the case of persons of German and Italian ancestry. See House Report No. 2124 (77th Cong., 2d Sess.) 247–52. It is asserted merely that the loyalties of this group "were unknown and time was of the essence." Yet nearly four months elapsed after Pearl Harbor before the first exclusion order was issued; nearly eight months went by until the last order was issued; and the last of these "subversive" persons was not actually removed until almost eleven months had elapsed. Leisure and deliberation seem to have been more of the essence than speed. And the fact that conditions were not such as to warrant a declaration of martial law adds strength to the belief that the factors of time and military necessity were not as urgent as they have been represented to be. . . .

I dissent, therefore, from this legalization of racism. Racial discrimination in any form and in any degree has no justifiable part whatever in our democratic way of life. It is unattractive in any setting but it is utterly revolting among a free people who have embraced the principles set forth in the Constitution of the United States. All residents of this nation are kin in some way by blood or culture to a foreign land. Yet they are primarily and necessarily a part of the new and distinct civilization of the United States. They must accordingly be treated at all times as the heirs of the American experiment and as entitled to all the rights and freedoms guaranteed by the Constitution.

## DISCUSSION QUESTIONS

1. Can you think of a law that might not pass the rationality test, a law that seems arbitrary and irrational?

2. If the independent butchers in the *Slaughter-House Cases* had proven that the real reason the Crescent City Live-stock Landing and Slaughter-House Company got a monopoly in New Orleans was because it bribed a large number of representatives in the Louisiana legislature, do you think the Court might have reached a different conclusion? Could you argue that a law that exists because of bribery violates the Equal Protection Clause or some other part of the Fourteenth Amendment?

3. One of the arguments against the separate but equal doctrine was that the facilities were never really equal. If they had been essentially equal,

should that have made a difference in the Court's decision to overturn this doctrine?

4. In *Plessy v. Ferguson* the majority of justices argued that laws that required different races to be treated differently in schools and railroad cars did not violate the principle of political equality. What do you think about that argument?

# CHAPTER
# three
❋ ❋ ❋ ❋ ❋ ❋ ❋ ❋

# Education and Racial Integration

.................................... DISCUSSION ............................................

The story of racial segregation in public schools really begins in 1850 with the decision by the Massachusetts Supreme Court in the case of *Roberts v. City of Boston*. A young black girl living in Boston was kept from attending the elementary school nearest her home because it was designated an all-white school. The Massachusetts statute on public education simply said that children should attend the school closest to their home unless special provisions were made. Nevertheless, the Massachusetts Supreme Court found nothing illegal about forcing this girl to travel an additional quarter of a mile to attend a public school for blacks. In the court's opinion, the schools were essentially "equal" except that the students were of different races. In this way, the concept of "separate but equal" public schools was born.

## SEPARATE BUT EQUAL AND THE FOURTEENTH AMENDMENT

For a long time after the Civil War and the passage of the Fourteenth Amendment, no one challenged the existence of separate but equal public schools. Finally, in 1896, a Louisiana "separate but equal" law was challenged. The law required railroads to provide "equal but separate accommodations" for "colored" and "white" passengers and made it a crime for members of either race to use railroad cars designated for the other race. Justice Miller wrote the decision in the case, *Plessy v. Ferguson* (see p. 23). Writing for the majority, Justice Miller made a distinction between "social" and "political" equality. He did not think the concept of equal protection meant that "schools, theaters, and railway carriages" had to be integrated. *Plessy v. Ferguson* arrived at the Supreme Court almost three decades after the ratification of the Fourteenth Amendment. Justice Miller emphasized that during that time many cities and states had operated "separate schools for colored children" and that this practice "does not seem to have been questioned."

In 1899 the Court demonstrated that, while it paid lip service to the doctrine of separate but equal in public education, it was not willing to enforce even this limited concept rigorously. In *Cummings v. Board of Education*, a school board in Georgia decided to close down the black high school and convert it to an elementary school for black children. This left the black children without a public high school. In a unanimous decision written by Justice Harlan, the Court only considered whether or not the white high school should be closed down until a new high school could be built for black children to ensure "equal" treatment. The Court decided that this would only deprive white children of an education without doing anything for black children. In the Court's opinion, the fact that black children had no public high school to attend did not violate the concept of equal protection.

During the 1930s and 1940s the National Association for the Advancement of Colored People (NAACP) decided that it would not challenge the doctrine of separate but equal directly but would instead challenge the lack of *actual* equality, particularly in public higher education. In 1938, in the case of *Missouri v. Canada*, Lloyd Gaines, a black man, had applied for admission to the state law school in Missouri. Missouri had no law school for blacks, but the state offered to pay Lloyd Gaines's tuition to attend a law school outside of Missouri that did admit blacks. Chief Justice Hughes, writing for the seven-justice majority, ruled that Missouri's action did not meet the requirements of the concept of separate but equal. Missouri would either have to provide a truly "equal" law school for blacks or admit Lloyd Gaines to the state law school.

A decade later Heman Sweatt asked to be admitted to the University of Texas Law School and was turned down because of his race. Texas, which had no law school for blacks, was given an opportunity to build one. Texas did build a law school just for blacks, and the federal district judge ruled that the new school was "substantially equivalent" to the law school for whites. In 1950, in *Sweatt v. Painter*, Chief Justice Vinson, writing for a unanimous Court, overturned the district court's decision, finding that the two schools were clearly not equal. The white law school had 16 full-time professors, 850 students, and 65,000 volumes in the law library, compared with the black law school, which had 5 full-time professors, 23 students, and 16,500 volumes in the law library. Because these two schools were not "substantially equal," the

Court ruled that Heman Sweatt had to be admitted to the all-white University of Texas Law School.

## THE END OF SEPARATE BUT EQUAL

In the 1950 case of *McLaurin v. Oklahoma State Regents*, the Court began to move away from the basic logic of *Plessy*. *McLaurin* involved a black graduate student, G. W. McLaurin, who was admitted to the University of Oklahoma under court order by a federal judge. The university then set up special rules for McLaurin. He was required to sit in a special seat in class, eat at a special time and at a particular table in the cafeteria, and otherwise use "for coloreds only" facilities. Chief Justice Vinson, writing for a unanimous Court, ruled that these state-imposed restrictions violated the Equal Protection Clause. Although they acknowledged that students still might choose, voluntarily, not to talk to or eat with McLaurin, the justices decided that there was a big difference between a state rule requiring segregation and a voluntary refusal of individual students to interact with other students. In *Plessy*, Justice Miller had emphasized that legislatures could not overcome "social prejudice" with legislation. Finally, in the 1950 *McLaurin* decision, a unanimous Court made a distinction between acknowledging the existence of social prejudice and passing laws that required racial separation.

Encouraged by this result, the NAACP Legal Defense and Educational Fund, with Thurgood Marshall as lead counsel (who was later appointed to the Supreme Court by President Johnson in 1967), decided to challenge the doctrine of separate but equal public schools. The case of *Brown v. Board of Education* (see p. 43) was argued and reargued before the Court over a period of two years. Finally, in 1954, Chief Justice Warren, writing for a unanimous Court, asked:

> Does segregation of children in public schools solely on the basis of race, even though the physical facilities and other "tangible" factors may be equal, deprive the children of the minority group of equal educational opportunities?

The unanimous Court decided that it did. Still, *Plessy* was not officially overruled. The Court simply decided that the concept of separate but equal "has no place" in public education. The justices accepted the argument that by segregating people the state was helping to create a "feeling of inferiority" and, for this reason, segregation violated the principle of equal protection.

## INTEGRATING THE PUBLIC SCHOOLS

The task of actually integrating public school systems proved to be very difficult. How could public school systems across the United States that had been set up since the Civil War on the basis of "separate but equal" be integrated? The justices postponed the question of how to do this until the next year. In 1955, with a decision that is commonly called *Brown v. Board of Education II*, the Court decided that segregated public school systems should be taken apart with "all deliberate speed." The justices hoped that school districts across the country would make a "reasonable start toward full compliance" and do whatever was required to reach full compliance "at the earliest practicable date." The problem with this decision was that it did not give any concrete guidance to either the school districts or the federal district judges who were expected to work out plans to integrate formerly segregated school systems. And no one was prepared for the storm of protest that resulted from the Court's decision.

Little Rock, Arkansas, became a symbol for both those who hoped to achieve integration and those who wished to avoid it. While school officials prepared a plan for desegregation, the Arkansas legislature passed laws that required segregation. The governor sent state police to prevent black children from entering the previously all-white high school. The federal district judge ordered the governor to stop, and finally President Eisenhower had to send in federal troops to enforce the order and protect black children who wanted to attend the high school. In 1958, in an unusual decision signed by all nine justices, the Supreme Court refused to give Little Rock any more time to comply with the district judge's order (*Cooper v. Aaron*).

## ALL DELIBERATE SPEED

The phrase "all deliberate speed" in the *Brown II* decision was taken to mean "not very fast" by many school officials around the country. School districts came up with a variety of plans to delay integration. Some proposed integrating a grade each year beginning with the first grade, so that children raised on segregation would not have to adjust to a completely new system. Other school districts tried to prevent integration by not providing necessary bus transportation. Finally, in 1969, the Supreme Court made it clear that the time for just "deliberate speed" had run out. In a per curiam decision in *Alexander v. Holmes County Board of Education*, the Supreme Court reviewed a decision by the Fifth Circuit Court of Appeals that would have allowed the county school system more time to integrate. The Court said that "all deliberate speed" was no longer "constitutionally permissible." Every school system that had operated a dual system based on race, the Court ruled, must terminate the dual system at once and operate an integrated school system.

## DE JURE VERSUS DE FACTO SEGREGATION

The courts developed a distinction between de jure and de facto segregation. *De jure*, meaning by law, segregation is segregation caused by school officials' decisions to either create or maintain racial segregation. On the other hand, *de facto*, meaning by the facts, segregation occurs where schools are segregated for reasons other than discriminatory decisions by government officials. In theory, a school system in which children simply attend their closest school, which happens to be populated mainly by children of one race because of segregated housing patterns, does not violate the principle of equal protection. At the same time, courts had to recognize that school officials could encourage segregation in many ways besides setting up a dual school system.

In 1973 the Supreme Court examined segregation in a major school system outside the South for the first time in *Keyes v. School District No. 1*. Unlike school districts in many southern states, the Denver school district had never been required by state law to separate the races. Nevertheless, the Supreme Court, in a decision written by Justice Brennan, ruled that a school system could be found to be operating a de jure segregated school system if there had been a "segregative purpose or intent" in the school board's decisions. In this case, the Court decided that the existence of racially segregated schools and a history of decisions by school authorities that helped to create schools in which black and Hispanic students predominated could constitute de jure segregation.

Justices Douglas and Powell each wrote concurring opinions in which they acknowledged the difficulty of deciding whether segregation was intentional or not. Justice Douglas argued that the existence of de facto segregation should be enough to justify orders to force integration. Justice Powell, the only justice to have served on a school board, argued that school officials in school districts with segregated schools should be required to prove they are operating a "genuinely integrated system." Only Justice Rehnquist dissented. The result of Justice Brennan's decision was that the Denver schools would be subjected to the same kind of supervision by a federal judge to bring about racial integration that schools in the South had endured for two decades.

The response from many middle-class white parents in school districts around the country was to move out of cities where their children would be forced to attend schools with a large number of minority children and into suburban school districts where the schools would be predominantly white.

## METHODS OF INTEGRATION

Deciding on how to integrate formerly segregated public schools was not easy. School districts tried a variety of tactics to avoid having to come up with methods that placed large numbers of students of different races in a single school. One tactic was the "grade-a-year" plan. In the 1950s and early 1960s, this was a popular way to avoid what some thought would be the "trauma" of having older children who had grown up with segregation suddenly thrown into schools with students of the other race. Finally, in a 1965 per curiam decision in *Rogers v. Paul,* the Supreme Court ruled that these plans were taking too long and that black high school students had a right to attend integrated public schools "immediately."

Another tactic was to implement "freedom-of-choice" plans. The idea was that any black student who wished to attend a white school would be free to do so, and vice versa. Of course, there was a great deal of social pressure to prevent this from actually happening. In 1968, with a decision in *Green v. County School Board,* the Court ruled that these plans were not sufficient unless they actually resulted in racially integrated schools. In this case, no white student had chosen to attend a formerly all-black school, and 85 percent of black students continued to attend all-black schools. In other words, freedom-of-choice might be an acceptable alternative if it actually resulted in racially integrated schools, but in this case it did not and the county school board would have to try something else. Justice Brennan, writing for the Court, stated that the burden on a school district was to "come forward with a plan that promises realistically to work, and promises realistically to work now."

Before the 1971 decision in *Swann v. Charlotte-Mecklenburg Board of Education,* the Supreme Court did not discuss in any detail how racial integration should be brought about. In *Swann,* Chief Justice Burger wrote the opinion for a unanimous Court. Almost 30 percent of the students in the Charlotte, North Carolina, school district were black. After years of supervision by a federal judge, the district remained basically segregated. The federal judge ultimately ordered busing between mainly white schools and mainly black schools, including elementary schools, to bring about racial integration. In reviewing the case, the chief justice began by saying that once de jure segregation had been proven, the "scope of a district court's equitable powers to remedy past wrongs is broad." He then approved the judge's redrawing of school attendance zones and forced busing to achieve racial integration.

## THE PROBLEM OF WHITE SUBURBAN SCHOOLS

The outrage by whites against forced racial integration was as great, if not greater, in many northern cities. Boston had worse riots over forced busing than any southern city. In Detroit, almost all the middle-class whites with school-age children had moved out of the city by the early 1970s, in part to avoid having their children attend integrated schools. The federal district judge in Detroit decided that the only way he could bring an end to racially segregated schools would be to order busing between the Detroit school district in the center and the surrounding suburban school districts.

The case of *Milliken v. Bradley* (see p. 47) appealed this decision to the Supreme Court in 1974. Chief Justice Burger framed the question of the case as

> whether a federal court may impose a multidistrict, areawide remedy to a single-district *de jure* segregation problem absent any finding that the other included school districts have failed to operate unitary school systems within their district, absent any claim or finding that the boundary lines of any affected school district were established with the purpose of fostering racial segregation in public schools, absent any finding that the included districts committed acts which effected segregation within the other districts, and absent a meaningful opportunity for the included neighboring school districts to present evidence or be heard on the propriety of a multidistrict remedy or on the question of constitutional violations by those neighboring districts.

The Court ruled, with a vote of five to four, that the answer to this question is no. Chief Justice Burger wrote the opinion for the majority. The federal district judge had realized that if he ordered busing inside the Detroit district he would only increase the white flight to the suburbs, which would certainly defeat the goal of racial integration. Instead, he planned to order the Detroit school district and 53 surrounding suburban school districts to develop a metropolitan plan for desegregation. The majority of justices believed this was beyond the power of a federal judge, absent any showing that these suburban school districts were in some way responsible for the segregation.

The four dissenting justices, Douglas, Brennan, White, and Marshall, all thought that once de jure racial segregation had been demonstrated a federal judge should be able to do whatever is necessary to bring about reasonable racial integration. They viewed the problem as one created by the state, not just one school district, and they viewed anything up to and including an entire statewide solution to be within the realm of legal possibility.

The practical result of the decision in *Milliken* was the creation of mostly minority central cities across the United States, surrounded by mostly white suburbs. During the 1970s, a massive migration of whites to the suburbs resulted in a very high level of segregation in both housing and public schools. Critics blamed the Supreme Court for this state of affairs. If in 1974 the Court had told white middle-class people that they could not escape the racial integration of public schools by moving to the suburbs, they might have stayed in the cities. Defenders of the Court argued that it is not the Court's job to be the ultimate social engineer for the society. Instead, it is the Court's job to end legally enforced segregation in public schools, a goal which had been essentially accomplished by the end of the 1980s.

## DEALING WITH WHITE FLIGHT

With white middle-class children concentrated in the suburbs and minority children concentrated in the inner cities, the question became one not of achieving racial integration, but of ensuring that minority children received a reasonable education. In the 1990 case of *Missouri v. Jenkins*, a federal district judge had ordered the state of Missouri and the Kansas City school district to spend an additional $450 million to upgrade schools for minority students. A variety of state laws prevented the district from raising taxes enough to comply with this order. The district judge ordered a significant increase in the property tax rate. The Supreme Court ruled that a federal judge could not raise the tax rate but could order the school board to raise the tax rate even though this would violate state law. Justice White wrote the opinion for the five-justice majority. He ruled that federal district judges have a great deal of power to fashion remedies to end racial segregation and states should not be allowed to "hinder the process by preventing a local government from implementing that remedy."

Justice Kennedy wrote a dissenting opinion, joined by Chief Justice Rehnquist and Justices O'Connor and Scalia. Justice Kennedy did not believe a federal judge should order this kind of remedy unless other remedies had been tried and failed.

## CONCLUSION

Beginning in 1954 the Supreme Court tried to move the United States away from segregated public schools. The Court met stiff resistance both from politicians and from millions of white middle-class citizens who were not willing to have their children attend integrated public schools. By the end of the 1980s, legally segregated public schools had essentially been eliminated from the United States. At the same time, most students attended public schools where either white children or minority children predominated. The dream of having most American children attend schools in which all the races learned together had not been fulfilled.

## CASE DECISIONS

The 1954 decision of *Brown v. Board of Education* consolidated several lawsuits brought by people representing black children who were required to attend segregated public schools. In a unanimous decision, Chief Justice Warren ruled that the concept of separate but equal had no place in public schools. Chief Justice Warren's opinion for the Court is included here in its entirety.

In the 1974 case of *Milliken v. Bradley*, the Court decided that, as a general rule, remedies for the racial segregation of public schools could not cross school district boundaries. Chief Justice Burger wrote the majority opinion, which is included here. Justice Stewart's concurring opinion is not included here. Four justices dissented and Justices Douglas, White, and Marshall wrote dissenting opinions, all of which are included here.

Following are excerpts from the case decisions.

❊ ❊ ❊ ❊ ❊ ❊ ❊ ❊ ❊

## BROWN v. BOARD OF EDUCATION
### 347 U.S. 483 (1954)

Mr. Chief Justice Warren delivered the opinion of the Court.

These cases come to us from the States of Kansas, South Carolina, Virginia, and Delaware. They are premised on different facts and different local conditions, but a common legal question justifies their consideration together in this consolidated opinion.

In each of the cases, minors of the Negro race, through their legal representatives, seek the aid of the courts in obtaining admission to the public schools of their community on a nonsegregated basis. In each instance, they have been denied admission to schools attended by white children under laws requiring or permitting segregation according to race. This segregation was alleged to deprive the plaintiffs of the equal protection of the laws under the Fourteenth Amendment. In each of the cases other than the Delaware case, a three-judge federal district court denied relief to the plaintiffs on the so-called "separate but equal" doctrine announced by this Court in *Plessy v. Ferguson*, 163 U.S. 537. Under that doctrine, equality of treatment is accorded when the races are provided substantially equal facilities, even though these facilities be separate. In the Delaware case, the Supreme Court of Delaware adhered to that doctrine, but ordered that the plaintiffs be admitted to the white schools because of their superiority to the Negro schools.

The plaintiffs contend that segregated public schools are not "equal" and cannot be made "equal," and that hence they are deprived of the equal protection of the laws. Because of the obvious importance of the question presented, the Court took jurisdiction. Argument was heard in the 1952 Term, and reargument was heard this Term on certain questions propounded by the Court.

Reargument was largely devoted to the circumstances surrounding the adoption of the Fourteenth Amendment in 1868. It covered exhaustively consideration of the Amendment in Congress, ratification by the states, then existing practices in racial segregation, and the views of proponents and opponents of the Amendment. This discussion and our own investigation convince us that, although these sources cast some light, it is not enough to resolve the problem with which we are faced. At best, they are inconclusive. The most avid proponents of the post-War Amendments undoubtedly in-tended them to remove all legal distinctions among "all persons born or naturalized in the United States." Their opponents, just as certainly, were antagonistic to both the letter and spirit of the Amendments and wished them to have the most limited effect. What others in Congress and the state legislatures had in mind cannot be determined with any degree of certainty.

An additional reason for the inconclusive nature of the Amendment's history, with respect to segregated schools, is the status of public education at that time. In the South, the movement toward free common schools, sup-ported by general taxation, had not yet taken hold. Education of white children was largely in the hands of private groups. Education of Negroes was almost nonexistent, and practically all of the race were illiterate. In fact, any education of Negroes was forbidden by law in some states. Today, in contrast, many Negroes have achieved outstanding success in the arts and sciences as well as in the business and professional world. It is true that public school education at the time of the Amendment had advanced further in the North, but the effect of the Amendment on Northern States was generally ignored in the congressional debates. Even in the North, the conditions of public education did not approximate those existing today. The curriculum was usually rudimentary; ungraded schools were common in rural areas; the school term was but three months a year in many states; and compulsory school attendance was virtually unknown. As a consequence, it is not surprising that there should be so little in the history of the Fourteenth Amendment relating to its intended effect on public education.

In the first cases in this Court construing the Fourteenth Amendment, decided shortly after its adoption, the Court interpreted it as proscribing all state-imposed discriminations against the Negro race. The doctrine of "separate but equal" did not make its appearance in this Court until 1896 in the case of *Plessy v. Ferguson, supra,* involving not education but transportation. American courts have since labored with the doctrine for over half a century. In this Court, there have been six cases involving the "separate but equal" doctrine in the field of public education. In *Cumming v. Board of Education of Richmond County,* 175 U.S. 528, and *Gong Lum v. Rice,* 275 U.S. 78, the validity of the doctrine itself was not challenged. In more recent cases, all on the graduate school level, inequality was found in that specific benefits enjoyed by white students were denied to Negro students of the same educational qualifications. *State of Missouri ex rel. Gaines v. Canada,* 305 U.S. 337; *Sipuel v. Board of Regents of University of Oklahoma,* 332 U.S. 631; *Sweatt v. Painter,* 339 U.S. 629; *McLaurin v. Oklahoma State Regents,* 339 U.S. 637. In none of these cases was it necessary to re-examine the doctrine to grant relief to the Negro plaintiff. And in *Sweatt v. Painter, supra,* the Court expressly reserved decision on the question whether *Plessy v. Ferguson* should be held inapplicable to public education.

In the instant cases, that question is directly presented. Here, unlike *Sweatt v. Painter,* there are findings that the Negro and white schools involved have been equalized, or are being equalized, with respect to buildings, curricula, qualifications and salaries of teachers, and other "tangible" factors. Our decision, therefore, cannot turn on merely a comparison of these tangible factors in the Negro and white schools involved in each of the cases. We must look instead to the effect of segregation itself on public education.

In approaching this problem, we cannot turn the clock back to 1868 when the Amendment was adopted, or even to 1896 when *Plessy v. Ferguson* was written. We must consider public education in the light of its full development and its present place in American life throughout the Nation. Only in this way can it be determined if segregation in public schools deprives these plaintiffs of the equal protection of the laws.

Today, education is perhaps the most important function of state and local governments. Compulsory school attendance laws and the great expenditures for education both demonstrate our recognition of the importance of education to our democratic society. It is required in the performance of our most basic public responsibilities, even service in the armed forces. It is the very foundation of good citizenship. Today it is a principal instrument in awakening the child to cultural values, in preparing him for later professional training, and in helping him to adjust normally to his environment. In these days, it is doubtful that any child may reasonably be expected to succeed in life if he is denied the opportunity of an education. Such an opportunity, where the state has undertaken to provide it, is a right which must be made available to all on equal terms.

We come then to the question presented: Does segregation of children in public schools solely on the basis of race, even though the physical facilities and other "tangible" factors may be equal, deprive the children of the minority group of equal educational opportunities? We believe that it does.

In *Sweatt v. Painter, supra,* in finding that a segregated law school for Negroes could not provide them equal educational opportunities, this Court relied in large part on "those qualities which are incapable of objective measurement but which make for greatness in a law school." In *McLaurin v. Oklahoma State Regents, supra,* the Court, in requiring that a Negro admitted to a white graduate school be treated like all other students, again resorted to intangible considerations: ". . . his ability to study, to engage in discussions and exchange views with other students, and, in general, to learn his profession." Such considerations apply with added force to children in grade and high schools. To separate them from others of similar age and qualifications solely because of their race generates a feeling of inferiority as to their status in the community that may affect their hearts and minds in a way unlikely ever to be undone. The effect of this separation on their educational opportunities was well stated by a finding in the Kansas case by a court which nevertheless felt compelled to rule against the Negro plaintiffs:

> "Segregation of white and colored children in public schools has a detrimental effect upon the colored children. The impact is greater when it has the sanction of the law; for the policy of separating the races is usually interpreted as denoting the inferiority of the negro group. A sense of inferiority affects the motivation of a child to learn. Segregation with the sanction of law, therefore, has a tendency to [retard] the educational and mental development of Negro children and to deprive them of some of the benefits they would receive in a racial[ly] integrated school system."

Whatever may have been the extent of psychological knowledge at the time of *Plessy v. Ferguson,* this finding is amply supported by modern authority. Any language in *Plessy v. Ferguson* contrary to this finding is rejected.

We conclude that in the field of public education the doctrine of "separate but equal" has no place. Separate educational facilities are inherently unequal. Therefore, we hold that the plaintiffs and others similarly situated for whom the actions have been brought are, by reason of the segregation complained of, deprived of equal protection of the laws guaranteed by the Fourteenth Amendment. This disposition makes unnecessary any discussion whether such segregation also violates the Due Process Clause of the Fourteenth Amendment.

Because these are class actions, because of the wide applicability of this decision, and because of the great variety of local conditions, the formulation of decrees in these cases presents problems of considerable complexity. On reargument, the consideration of appropriate relief was necessarily subordinated to the primary question—the constitutionality of segregation in public education. We have now announced that such segregation is a denial of the equal protection of the laws. In order that we may have the full assistance of the parties in formulating decrees, the cases will be restored to the docket, and the parties are requested to present further argument on Questions 4 and 5 previously propounded by the Court for the reargument this Term. The Attorney General of the United States is again invited to participate. The Attorneys General of the states requiring or permitting segregation in public education will also be permitted to appear as *amici curiae* upon request to do so by September 15, 1954, and submission of briefs by October 1, 1954.

It is so ordered.

## MILLIKEN v. BRADLEY
### *418 U.S. 717 (1974)*

MR. CHIEF JUSTICE BURGER delivered the opinion of the Court.

We granted certiorari in these consolidated cases to determine whether a federal court may impose a multidistrict, areawide remedy to a single-district *de jure* segregation problem absent any finding that the other included school districts have failed to operate unitary school systems within their districts, absent any claim or finding that the boundary lines of any affected school district were established with the purpose of fostering racial segregation in public schools, absent any finding that the included districts committed acts which effected segregation within the other districts, and absent a meaningful opportunity for the included neighboring school districts to present evidence or be heard on the propriety of a multidistrict remedy or on the question of constitutional violations by those neighboring districts. . . .

Ever since *Brown v. Board of Education,* 347 U.S. 483 (1954), judicial consideration of school desegregation cases has begun with the standard:

"[I]n the field of public education the doctrine of 'separate but equal' has no place. Separate educational facilities are inherently unequal." *Id.,* at 495.

This has been reaffirmed time and again as the meaning of the Constitution and the controlling rule of law.

The target of the *Brown* holding was clear and forthright: the elimination of state-mandated or deliberately maintained dual school systems with certain schools for Negro pupils and others for white pupils. . . .

Here the District Court's approach to what constitutes "actual desegregation" raises the fundamental question, not presented in *Swann,* as to the circumstances in which a federal court may order desegregation relief that embraces more than a single school district. The court's analytical starting point was its conclusion that school district lines are no more than arbitrary lines on a map drawn "for political convenience." Boundary lines may be bridged where there has been a constitutional violation calling for interdistrict relief, but the notion that school district lines may be casually ignored or treated as a mere administrative convenience is contrary to the history of public education in our country. No single tradition in public education is more deeply rooted than local control over the operation of schools; local autonomy has long been thought essential both to the maintenance of community concern and support for public schools and to quality of the educational process. See *Wright v. Council of the City of Emporia,* 407 U.S., at 469. Thus, in *San Antonio School District v. Rodriguez,* 411 U.S. 1, 50 (1973), we observed that local control over the educational process affords citizens an opportunity to participate in decisionmaking, permits the structuring of school programs to fit local needs, and encourages "experimentation, innovation, and a healthy competition for educational excellence."

The Michigan educational structure involved in this case, in common with most States, provides for a large measure of local control, and a review of the scope and character of these local powers indicates the extent to which the interdistrict remedy approved by the two courts could disrupt and alter the structure of public education in Michigan. The metropolitan remedy would require, in effect, consolidation of 54 independent school districts historically administered as separate units into a vast new super school district. See n. 10, *supra.* Entirely apart from the logistical and other serious problems attending large-scale transportation of students, the consolidation would give rise to an array of other problems in financing and operating this new school system. Some of the more obvious questions would be: What would be the status and authority of the present popularly elected school boards? Would the children of Detroit be within the jurisdiction and operating control of a school board elected by the parents and residents of other districts? What board or boards would levy taxes for school operations in these 54 districts constituting the consolidated metropolitan area? What provisions could be made for assuring substantial equality in tax levies among the 54 districts, if this were deemed requisite? What provisions would be made for financing? Would the validity of long-term bonds be jeopardized unless approved by all of the component districts as well as the State? What body would determine that portion of the curricula now left to the discretion of local school boards? Who would establish attendance zones, purchase school equipment, locate and construct new schools, and indeed attend to all the myriad day-to-day decisions that are necessary to school operations affecting potentially more than three-quarters of a million pupils? . . .

The controlling principle consistently expounded in our holdings is that the scope of the remedy is determined by the nature and extent of the constitutional violation. *Swann*, 402 U.S., at 16. Before the boundaries of separate and autonomous school districts may be set aside by consolidating the separate units for remedial purposes or by imposing a cross-district remedy, it must first be shown that there has been a constitutional violation within one district that produces a significant segregative effect in another district. Specifically, it must be shown that racially discriminatory acts of the state or local school districts, or of a single school district have been a substantial cause of interdistrict segregation. Thus an interdistrict remedy might be in order where the racially discriminatory acts of one or more school districts caused racial segregation in an adjacent district, or where district lines have been deliberately drawn on the basis of race. In such circumstances an interdistrict remedy would be appropriate to eliminate the interdistrict segregation directly caused by the constitutional violation. Conversely, without an interdistrict violation and interdistrict effect, there is no constitutional wrong calling for an interdistrict remedy.

The record before us, voluminous as it is, contains evidence of *de jure* segregated conditions only in the Detroit schools; indeed, that was the theory on which the litigation was initially based and on which the District Court took evidence. See *supra*, at 725–726. With no showing of significant violation by the 53 outlying school districts and no evidence of any interdistrict violation or effect, the court went beyond the original theory of the case as framed by the pleadings and mandated a metropolitan area remedy. . . .

The constitutional right of the Negro respondents residing in Detroit is to attend a unitary school system in that district. Unless petitioners drew the district lines in a discriminatory fashion, or arranged for white students residing in the Detroit District to attend schools in Oakland and Macomb Counties, they were under no constitutional duty to make provisions for Negro students to do so. The view of the dissenters, that the existence of a dual system in *Detroit* can be made the basis for a decree requiring cross-district transportation of pupils cannot be supported on the grounds that it represents merely the devising of a suitably flexible remedy for the violation of rights already established by our prior decisions. It can be supported only by drastic expansion of the constitutional right itself, an expansion without any support in either constitutional principle or precedent.

**Dissenting Opinion**   MR. JUSTICE DOUGLAS, dissenting.

Here the Michigan educational system is unitary, maintained and supported by the legislature and under the general supervision of the State Board of Education. The State controls the boundaries of school districts. The State supervises schoolsite selection. The construction is done through municipal bonds approved by several state agencies. Education in Michigan is a state project with very little completely local control, except that the schools are financed locally, not on a statewide basis. Indeed the proposal to put school funding in Michigan on a statewide basis was defeated at the polls in November 1972. Yet the school districts by state law are agencies of the State. State action is indeed challenged as violating the Equal Protection Clause. Whatever the reach of that claim may be, it certainly is aimed at discrimination based on race.

Therefore as the Court of Appeals held there can be no doubt that as a matter of Michigan law the State itself has the final say as to where and how school district lines should be drawn.

When we rule against the metropolitan area remedy we take a step that will likely put the problems of the blacks and our society back to the period that antedated the "separate but equal" regime of *Plessy v. Ferguson*, 163 U.S. 537. The reason is simple.

The inner core of Detroit is now rather solidly black; and the blacks, we know, in many instances are likely to be poorer, just as were the Chicanos in *San Antonio School District v. Rodriguez*, 411 U.S. 1. By that decision the poorer school districts must pay their own way. It is therefore a foregone conclusion that we have now given the States a formula whereby the poor must pay their own way.

Today's decision, given *Rodriguez*, means that there is no violation of the Equal Protection Clause though the schools are segregated by race and though the black schools are not only "separate" but "inferior." . . .

**Dissenting Opinion**   MR. JUSTICE WHITE, with whom MR. JUSTICE DOUGLAS, MR. JUSTICE BRENNAN, and MR. JUSTICE MARSHALL join, dissenting.

The District Court and the Court of Appeals found that over a long period of years those in charge of the Michigan public schools engaged in various practices calculated to effect the segregation of the Detroit school system. The Court does not question these findings, nor could it reasonably do so. Neither does it question the obligation of the federal courts to devise a feasible and effective remedy. But it promptly cripples the ability of the judiciary to perform this task, which is of fundamental importance to our constitutional system, by fashioning a strict rule that remedies in school cases must stop at the school district line unless certain other conditions are met. As applied here, the remedy for unquestioned violations of the equal protection rights of Detroit's Negroes by the Detroit School Board and the State of Michigan must be totally confined to the limits of the school district and may not reach into adjoining or surrounding districts unless and until it is proved there has been some sort of "interdistrict violation"—unless unconstitutional actions of the Detroit School Board have had a segregative impact on other districts, or unless the segregated condition of the Detroit schools has itself been influenced by segregative practices in those surrounding districts into which it is proposed to extend the remedy.

Regretfully, and for several reasons, I can join neither the Court's judgment nor its opinion. The core of my disagreement is that deliberate acts of segregation and their consequences will go unremedied, not because a remedy would be infeasible or unreasonable in terms of the usual criteria governing school desegregation cases, but because an effective remedy would cause what the Court considers to be undue administrative inconvenience to the State. The result is that the State of Michigan, the entity at which the Fourteenth Amendment is directed, has successfully insulated itself from its duty to provide effective desegregation remedies by vesting sufficient power over its public schools in its local school districts. If this is the case in Michigan, it will be the case in most States.

**Dissenting Opinion**   MR. JUSTICE MARSHALL, with whom MR. JUSTICE DOUGLAS, MR. JUSTICE BRENNAN, and MR. JUSTICE WHITE join, dissenting.

In *Brown v. Board of Education*, 347 U.S. 483 (1954), this Court held that segregation of children in public schools on the basis of race deprives minority group children of equal educational opportunities and therefore denies them the equal protection of the laws under the Fourteenth Amendment. This Court recognized then that remedying decades of segregation in public education would not be an easy task. Subsequent events, unfortunately, have seen that prediction bear bitter fruit. But however imbedded old ways, however ingrained old prejudices, this Court has not been diverted from its appointed task of making "a living truth" of our constitutional ideal of equal justice under law. *Cooper v. Aaron,* 358 U.S. 1, 20 (1958).

After 20 years of small, often difficult steps toward that great end, the Court today takes a giant step backwards. Notwithstanding a record showing widespread and pervasive racial segregation in the educational system provided by the State of Michigan for children in Detroit, this Court holds that the District Court was powerless to require the State to remedy its constitutional violation in any meaningful fashion. Ironically purporting to base its result on the principle that the scope of the remedy in a desegregation case should be determined by the nature and the extent of the constitutional violation, the Court's answer is to provide no remedy at all for the violation proved in this case, thereby guaranteeing that Negro children in Detroit will receive the same separate and inherently unequal education in the future as they have been unconstitutionally afforded in the past.

I cannot subscribe to this emasculation of our constitutional guarantee of equal protection of the laws and must respectfully dissent. Our precedents, in my view, firmly establish that where, as here, state-imposed segregation has been demonstrated, it becomes the duty of the State to eliminate root and branch all vestiges of racial discrimination and to achieve the greatest possible degree of actual desegregation. I agree with both the District Court and the Court of Appeals that, under the facts of this case, this duty cannot be fulfilled unless the State of Michigan involves outlying metropolitan area school districts in its desegregation remedy. Furthermore, I perceive no basis either in law or in the practicalities of the situation justifying the State's interposition of school district boundaries as absolute barriers to the implementation of an effective desegregation remedy. Under established and frequently used Michigan procedures, school district lines are both flexible and permeable for a wide variety of purposes, and there is no reason why they must now stand in the way of meaningful desegregation relief.

The rights at issue in this case are too fundamental to be abridged on grounds as superficial as those relied on by the majority today. We deal here with the right of all of our children, whatever their race, to an equal start in life and to an equal opportunity to reach their full potential as citizens. Those children who have been denied that right in the past deserve better than to see fences thrown up to deny them that right in the future. Our Nation, I fear, will be ill served by the Court's refusal to remedy separate and unequal education, for unless our children begin to learn together, there is little hope that our people will ever learn to live together. . . .

Because of the already high and rapidly increasing percentage of Negro students in the Detroit system, as well as the prospect of white flight, a Detroit-only plan simply has no hope of achieving actual desegregation. Under such a plan white and Negro students will not go to school together. Instead, Negro children will continue to attend all-Negro schools. The very evil that *Brown I* was aimed at will not be cured, but will be perpetuated for the future. . . .

## .................................DISCUSSION QUESTIONS.................................

1. In the 1950s, when the Supreme Court decided that separate but equal had no place in public education, some people believed that the first step to school integration should have been to upgrade the black schools so that they were clearly superior to the white schools in cities across the United States. These people argued that white parents would go along with this plan if it allowed their children to remain in all-white public schools. Once black schools were clearly superior, students in the district would be allowed to decide which school they wished to attend. If this plan had been followed, do you think it would have made any difference in the history of school integration in the United States? Could a school district, after 1954, have intentionally engaged in a plan to make black schools clearly superior to white schools without violating the Equal Protection Clause?

2. The NAACP waited until the 1950s to argue that separate but equal should no longer apply to public school education in the United States. Why do you think the NAACP waited to bring this issue to the Supreme Court? Do you think the NAACP was right to wait? In your opinion, would the New Deal Court have reached the same conclusion in the early 1940s? If the Court had made the decision in the early 1940s and demanded immediate integration, do you think it might have been easier for the society to integrate while fighting World War II? Do you think the Court might have refused to order such a drastic change in society given the strain the country was already going through trying to win the war?

3. Although the Court talked about separate but equal, black public schools were clearly inferior to white public schools in many parts of the United States. The Court's decision in *Cummings* demonstrated

that the Court was not very serious about enforcing the "equal" part of separate but equal. If the Court had demanded that every aspect of public education be equal, from the size and quality of the buildings to the qualifications of the faculty, do you think segregation would have been acceptable? Why or why not?

4. The controversial *Milliken* decision was five to four against allowing a federal district judge to order the city of Detroit to join with surrounding suburban school districts to bring about racial integration in area public schools. Do you agree with the Court's decision? Why or why not? Do you think this is an issue for Congress or the Supreme Court to address?

# CHAPTER
## four

❖ ❖ ❖ ❖ ❖ ❖ ❖ ❖ ❖

# Affirmative Action

······················· DISCUSSION ·······························

A ffirmative action has been a difficult issue for both the Supreme
Court and society. Generally, when people speak about affirmative
action, they mean giving people from particular groups special consideration. Some justices, and some groups in society, believe that governments at all levels should be allowed great freedom in developing plans to
make up for past racial discrimination. Other justices, and other groups in
society, have argued that an affirmative action plan is nothing more than
open, obvious discrimination based on race (against whites) and therefore
should not be allowed unless there is a compelling reason for it.

Looking at decisions since the mid-1970s, when affirmative action plans
began to be seriously challenged, we can see quite clearly that each justice
has had a particular view about when affirmative action plans based on race
should or should not be allowed. As justices have been replaced, new justices
join the Court with their own opinions about affirmative action, adding to
the uncertainty in an already uncertain area of the law. We might have a
good idea of what Justices Brennan, White, Marshall, Powell, and Blackmun
thought about these plans, but all five of these justices are no longer on the
Court. In most affirmative action cases, a majority of justices have not been
able to agree on why a particular affirmative action plan was or was not
acceptable, so later justices can have a significant impact on this "unsettled"
area of constitutional law.

In this chapter we will discuss only affirmative action plans designed to
give preferences based on race and instituted by federal, state, or local

government. Affirmative action plans based on sex will be discussed in chapter 6.

The Court has divided affirmative action plans into two basic groups: quota plans and race-plus plans. Under a quota plan, a government considers members of a particular race separately from members of other races and uses different criteria in determining whether the people of this particular race get a government benefit, such as admission to a state university, a government job, or a government license. In these plans there is usually a "quota," based on the percentage of people of the target racial group in the population, and an effort is made to grant the benefit to a particular percentage of people until the quota is met. For example, if 10 percent of a state's population is Hispanic, the state might try to make sure that 10 percent of every entering class in the state law school is also Hispanic. A race-plus plan does not place people of different races into different groups. Instead, particular racial characteristics are considered to be a plus in making the final decision as to who does and who does not receive the government benefit.

## AFFIRMATIVE ACTION BY STATE UNIVERSITIES

In 1978 the Supreme Court handed down its first decision concerning affirmative action plans. The case, *Regents of the University of California v. Bakke* (see p. 64), involved a white man, Allan Bakke, who had applied for admission to, and been rejected by, the University of California at Davis Medical School in 1973 and 1974. The university had an affirmative action plan that set a quota of 16 "black, Hispanic, and Asian" students for every entering class of 100. For the rest of the 3,000 applicants, college grades and scores on the MCAT (a national medical school entrance exam) formed the basis for admission decisions. Allan Bakke objected when he found out that he had been turned down while minority students with lower college grades and MCAT scores had been admitted under the university's affirmative action plan.

The Court divided into three groups. Four justices favored admitting Allan Bakke because, in their opinion, quota affirmative action plans violated Title VI of the 1964 Civil Rights Act. (This section of the 1964 Civil Rights Act outlawed racial discrimination by educational institutions receiving federal funds and did not discuss affirmative action. The University of California received federal funds.) Four justices were against admitting Allan Bakke. Justice Powell was the swing vote, so his decision became the decision of the Court.

Justice Powell declared that Allan Bakke would be admitted to the medical school because the University of California's affirmative action plan, as written, violated the Equal Protection Clause of the Fourteenth Amendment. Because the discrimination in this case was based on race, Justice Powell agreed that "strict scrutiny" must be used in making a decision. The university's affirmative action plan clearly treated people differently because of their race, so a compelling reason would have to be put forward to justify this racial discrimination. In Justice Powell's opinion, the Fourteenth Amendment is framed in "universal terms" and must be interpreted to protect everyone, even white males, against discrimination based on race. Justice Powell refused to accept the idea that discrimination against whites was somehow different from discrimination against blacks or other minorities.

Justice Powell also argued that there are "serious problems of justice connected with the idea of preference, such as the preference used in affirmative action programs." First, it is not always clear what constitutes a preference. Second, any kind of preferential program is likely to "reinforce common stereotypes holding that certain groups are unable to achieve success without special protection based on a factor having no relationship to individual worth." Third, there is at least some inequity in forcing people such as Allan Bakke to bear the burden for correcting past injustices when they themselves are not responsible for those injustices. Justice Powell concluded that people who are asked to bear a burden at the hands of government because of race have a right to ask that that burden be "precisely tailored to serve a compelling governmental" interest.

Justice Powell then examined the reasons given by the university to justify its affirmative action plan. First, the university argued that historically minorities had been discriminated against by medical schools. He concluded that the Supreme Court had never allowed racial preference to be used to overcome past discrimination without "judicial, legislative, or administrative findings" of past discrimination by a particular governmental unit. There were no such findings in this case. The university's second argument was that the plan was needed to overcome the effects of societal discrimination. Justice Powell did not think this reason was compelling enough to justify racial discrimination against white applicants. The university then argued that the plan was needed to improve the delivery of health care services in communities that lacked proper health care. Justice Powell could find no evidence in the record that racial discrimination against white applicants would help to overcome this problem.

The university's fourth argument was that it wanted to create a better learning environment by having a diverse student body. Justice Powell did accept the idea that a desire to attain a "diverse student body" was a "constitutionally permissible goal for an institution of higher education." He agreed that a diverse student body would add to the educational environ-ment, but he rejected the use of a strict quota system as a legitimate way to achieve this diversity. He pointed out:

> The diversity that furthers a compelling state interest encompasses a far broader array of qualifications and characteristics of which racial or ethnic origin is but a single though important element. Petitioner's special admissions program, focused solely on ethnic diversity, would hinder rather than further attainment of genuine diversity.

Justice Powell suggested that race, and other factors, could be taken into account and "deemed a plus" when making admission decisions. However, the current system of insulating some individuals from comparison with other candidates was unconstitutional. Other factors besides race that might be considered a plus include:

> exceptional personal talents, unique work or service experience, leader-ship potential, maturity, demonstrated compassion, a history of overcom-ing disadvantage, ability to communicate with the poor, or other qualifi-cations deemed important.

Justice Powell rejected the use of a strict quota plan and ordered Allan Bakke admitted to the University of California at Davis Medical School.

Justice Brennan's opinion, concurring in part and dissenting in part, was joined by Justices White, Marshall, and Blackmun. He argued that the university's current affirmative action plan did not violate the Equal Protec-tion Clause. He thought that the desire of the university to remedy the effects of past discrimination by society in general was a compelling enough reason to justify this kind of affirmative action plan.

Justice Stevens's opinion, concurring in part and dissenting in part, was joined by Chief Justice Burger and Justices Stewart and Rehnquist. Justice Stevens believed that the kind of discussion engaged in by Justice Powell was inappropriate. Justice Stevens would have simply ordered the university to admit Allan Bakke and left any discussion about what kinds of affirmative action plans "might" meet the requirements of the Equal Protection Clause to another day. In his opinion, Title VI of the 1964 Civil Rights Act outlawed racial discrimination by any institution receiving federal funds. The University of California received federal funds. He argued that Congress had made no provision for affirmative action plans in Title VI and such plans would be illegal until Congress addressed this problem.

The final result of the decision in *Bakke* was that the university was ordered to admit Allan Bakke and to stop using its quota-based affirmative action plan. Justice Powell presented his idea of what kind of affirmative action plan might withstand challenge, but his statements were essentially dicta, meaning they were only his opinion and did not carry the weight of the Court. Technically, none of the other justices joined that part of his opinion. The four justices who agreed that Allan Bakke should be admitted disagreed with Justice Powell's reasoning. The other four justices did not agree that Allan Bakke should be admitted. Nevertheless, many people, including members of the federal Department of Education, accepted Justice Powell's analysis as a statement of how an affirmative action plan by a state university could comply with the Equal Protection Clause.

## AFFIRMATIVE ACTION BY PUBLIC EMPLOYERS

In 1986, with *Wygant v. Jackson Board of Education*, the Court faced an affirmative action plan involving a school district. As the result of a lawsuit, the Jackson school district and the plaintiffs representing minorities had agreed to create an affirmative action plan to hire more minority teachers. When financial problems forced the school board to lay off employees, the board took steps to avoid laying off the newly hired minority teachers. The board implemented a plan that would have forced white teachers with more seniority to be laid off instead. These white teachers sued to stop this from happening, and their suit reached the Supreme Court. The Court ruled that these white teachers could not be laid off in violation of the seniority rules of the school district.

Justice Powell wrote the opinion for the Court, joined by Chief Justice Burger and Justice Rehnquist. Justice Powell asked what compelling reason justified this particular racial discrimination. The school district argued that minority teachers were needed to provide role models for minority students and that the affirmative action plan would also help to overcome general racial discrimination in society. Justice Powell said that these two reasons were not "compelling" enough to justify racial discrimination. He also thought that the idea of overcoming "societal discrimination, without more, is too amorphous a basis for imposing a racially classified remedy."

Justice O'Connor wrote a concurring opinion in which she agreed that the "role model" and "societal discrimination" justifications were not compelling enough to justify using an affirmative action plan. For her, the only reason that justified this kind of racial discrimination was to overcome past intentional racial discrimination.

Justice White's concurring opinion drew a major distinction between not hiring a white employee and firing a white employee. In this case white employees were being laid off, in violation of a seniority plan, because of their race. He thought this was unreasonable. In his opinion, being laid off was a much greater burden than not being hired for a job in the first place, and people should not have to bear this burden for the sake of affirmative action.

Justices Marshall, Brennan, Blackmun, and Stevens dissented. In his dissenting opinion, Justice Marshall argued that a school district should be able to protect the gains that had been made in minority hiring by not laying off newly hired minority workers. Justice Stevens argued that the "role model" justification was compelling enough to justify this kind of affirmative action by a school district.

In 1987, with *United States v. Paradise*, a majority of justices upheld a court-ordered affirmative action plan that required the state of Alabama to promote one black state trooper to the rank of corporal for every white trooper promoted until the percentage of black corporals in the state police reached 25 percent. The state police of Alabama had been operating under court orders for many years to integrate the police force, and the state had resisted every step of the way. The federal district judge found that the state had engaged in intentional racial discrimination in both hiring and promotions and that this kind of quota plan was the only way to overcome past intentional discrimination. Justice Powell was again the swing vote, and he accepted this court-ordered quota plan because it met his personal list of criteria. He thought quota plans were justified to overcome past intentional discrimination if

1. there was no real alternative remedy,
2. the plan was of a fixed duration,
3. the quota could be waived by the judge if the quota could not be met in good faith,
4. the percentage of minority hiring bore a reasonable relationship to the relevant labor pool,
5. the plan did not lay off any white employees.

Justice O'Connor dissented, joined by Chief Justice Rehnquist and Justice Scalia. She believed this remedy was not "narrowly tailored" enough to meet the strict scrutiny test. Justice White also dissented.

These and other sharply divided decisions in the 1980s left most government employers confused about when they could and could not engage in affirmative action and what type of affirmative action plan met the requirements of the Equal Protection Clause.

## AFFIRMATIVE ACTION FOR GOVERNMENT CONTRACTORS

In 1980 the Court faced a congressional affirmative action plan involving government contracts with businesses for public works projects. The case of *Fullilove v. Klutznick*, involved a law passed by Congress which required that 10 percent of federal funds granted for local public works projects be paid to businesses owned by members of specified minority groups. Six justices agreed that Congress had the power under the Fourteenth Amendment to order this kind of affirmative action plan.

Chief Justice Burger wrote the opinion for the Court, and his opinion was joined by Justices White and Powell. The chief justice agreed that a government program with "racial or ethnic criteria" required "close examination," but he also believed that the Court was required to show "appropriate deference" to Congress because the Fourteenth Amendment gave Congress the power to enforce the provisions of the amendment with "appropriate legislation." He found that Congress had a great deal of evidence to show that minority businesses had been denied effective participation in public contracting opportunities in the past and that current practices perpetuated this discrimination. Chief Justice Burger thought that "no organ of government" had the vast powers to remedy the effects of past discrimination that Congress had been given by the Fourteenth Amendment. In his opinion, the minority set-aside program was a "limited and properly tailored remedy to cure the effects of prior discrimination" and did not violate the Fourteenth Amendment.

Justice Powell, in his concurring opinion, argued that the need to overcome the "continuing effects of past discrimination" was a compelling enough reason to justify this particular affirmative action plan. Justices Marshall, Brennan, and Blackmun agreed with the result of the decision.

Justices Stewart, Rehnquist, and Stevens dissented. Justices Stewart and Rehnquist rejected the idea that anything could justify racial discrimination, even if the discrimination was part of an affirmative action plan approved by Congress. Justice Stevens questioned the list of people who would benefit from this plan. The list included "citizens of the United States who are Negroes, Spanish-speaking, Orientals, Indians, Eskimos, and Aleuts." There was nothing in the record to demonstrate how Congress arrived at this particular list. There was nothing to demonstrate what "common characteristics" Congress believed the members of the "preferred class" shared. He also did not find anything in the record to suggest how Congress arrived at the 10 percent figure.

In 1989 the Court examined a similar plan by the city of Richmond, Virginia, and found that it violated the Equal Protection Clause. The case, *Richmond v. J.A. Croson Co.* (see p. 71), involved a city plan patterned after the congressional plan discussed in *Fullilove*. The Richmond city plan required prime contractors to whom the city awarded construction contracts to subcontract at least 30 percent of the contract to one or more minority-owned businesses. This requirement did not apply to minority-owned prime contractors. The minorities who qualified were "Negro, Spanish-speaking, Oriental, Indian, Eskimo, or Aleut" people. A white contractor objected, arguing that the plan was simply racial discrimination, and the Supreme Court agreed with him.

In her opinion for the Court, joined by Chief Justice Rehnquist and Justice White, Justice O'Connor found the plan to be a violation of the Equal Protection Clause. She drew a distinction between the powers of Congress to "redress the effects of society-wide discrimination" and the powers of state and local governments. Although Congress had special powers in this regard, state and local governments certainly did not. She pointed out that the Fourteenth Amendment was specifically intended to be a "constraint" on state power in the area of racial discrimination.

At the same time, Justice O'Connor thought that a state or local government could take steps to "eradicate the effects of private discrimination." She stated:

> [I]f the city could show that it had essentially become a "passive participant" in a system of racial exclusion practiced by elements of the local construction industry, we think it clear that the city could take affirmative steps to dismantle such a system. It is beyond dispute that any public entity, state or federal, has a compelling interest in assuring that public dollars, drawn from the tax contributions of all citizens, do not serve to finance the evil of private prejudice.

She then subjected the process by which Richmond developed its plan to strict scrutiny and found it lacking. The city had not engaged in any kind of extensive fact-finding effort. Instead, Richmond based its ordinance on "an amorphous claim" that there had been discrimination in the construction industry. She found any estimate of the effect of this past discrimination to be "sheer speculation." In her opinion, the 30 percent quota was not based on any "realistic" judgment of harm. The city did not even know how many minorities were "qualified to undertake prime or subcontracting work in public construction projects." There was little concrete evidence concerning past discrimination against blacks, and there was "*absolutely no evidence of* past discrimination against Spanish-speaking, Oriental, Indian, Eskimo or Aleut persons in any aspect of the Richmond construction industry."

Justice Stevens, in his concurring opinion, pointed out that the city council in Richmond had "merely engaged in the type of stereotypical analysis that is a hallmark of violations" of the Equal Protection Clause. Justice Scalia, in his concurring opinion, called upon the Court to strike down all preferences based on race except for those necessary to provide a remedy to victims of unlawful past discrimination. He believed that "nothing prevents Richmond from according a contracting preference to identified victims of discrimination." He also thought that cities and states could move to help the "disadvantaged" without regard to race and that "since blacks have been disproportionately disadvantaged by racial discrimination, any race-neutral remedial program aimed at the disadvantaged as such will have a disproportionately beneficial impact on blacks." Justice Kennedy, in his concurring opinion, accepted Justice O'Connor's view that racial preference could be allowed only if it withstood the "most rigorous scrutiny by the courts."

Justices Brennan, Marshall, and Blackmun dissented. Justice Marshall argued that the desire to "eradicate" the effects of past discrimination and to stop the "perpetuation" of that past discrimination justified Richmond's plan. Justice Blackmun believed that the Court had regressed, and he hoped that one day it would "do its best to fulfill the great promises" of the Constitution.

## CONCLUSION

No other area of equal protection decision making has divided the Court as much as the area of affirmative action. Many important affirmative action decisions have been divided five to four, or rather four to four to one. In no other area have so many justices invoked their own personal set of criteria in determining whether or not a particular action violated the Fourteenth Amendment. Because of this, it is very difficult for attorneys, judges, and the society at large to know what the law is regarding affirmative action.

Affirmative action has caused a great deal of social controversy. Some people have passionately argued that two wrongs do not make a right, while others have just as passionately argued that only affirmative action, at least for some period of time, can correct the effects of so long a period of racial discrimination. Throughout this debate Congress has been strangely silent. While many of the justices believe that Congress has extraordinary powers to use affirmative action to remedy the effects of past racial discrimination, it has not done so with the exception of a few minority set-aside programs, such as those discussed in the *Fullilove* decision. Congress has refused to provide guidelines for cities and states to follow in this crucial area.

## ·····························CASE DECISIONS·····························

The first major affirmative action decision was the 1978 decision in *Regents of the University of California v. Bakke*. The Court divided into two groups of four justices, with Justice Powell as the swing vote. Because he was the swing vote, Justice Powell wrote the opinion for the Court, which is included here. Justices Brennan, White, Marshall, Stevens, and Blackmun wrote opinions which are not included here.

In 1989 a majority of the justices declared the affirmative action plan of Richmond, Virginia, to be a violation of the Equal Protection Clause in *Richmond v. J.A. Croson Co.* Justice O'Connor wrote the opinion for the Court, which is included here. Justices Stevens, Kennedy, and Scalia wrote concurring opinions, which are not included. Justices Marshall and Blackmun wrote dissenting opinions, which are not included.

Following are excerpts from the case decisions.

❋ ❋ ❋ ❋ ❋ ❋ ❋ ❋ ❋

## REGENTS OF THE UNIVERSITY OF CALIFORNIA v. BAKKE
### 438 U.S. 265 (1978)

MR. JUSTICE POWELL announced the judgment of the Court.

This case presents a challenge to the special admissions program of the petitioner, the Medical School of the University of California at Davis, which is designed to assure the admission of a specified number of students from certain minority groups. The Superior Court of California sustained respondent's challenge, holding that petitioner's program violated the California Constitution, Title VI of the Civil Rights Act of 1964, 42 U.S.C. § 2000d *et seq.*, and the Equal Protection Clause of the Fourteenth Amendment. The court enjoined petitioner from considering respondent's race or the race of any other applicant in making admissions decisions. It refused, however, to order respondent's admission to the Medical School, holding that he had not carried his burden of proving that he would have been admitted but for the constitutional and statutory violations. The Supreme Court of California affirmed those portions of the trial court's judgment decision declaring the special admissions program unlawful and enjoining petitioner from considering the race of any applicant. It modified that portion of the judgment denying respondent's requested injunction and directed the trial court to order his admission.

For reasons stated in the following opinion, I believe that so much of the judgment of the California court as holds petitioner's special admissions program unlawful and directs that respondent be admitted to the Medical School must be affirmed. For the reasons expressed in a separate opinion, my Brothers The Chief Justice, Mr. Justice Stewart, Mr. Justice Rehnquist and Mr. Justice Stevens concur in this judgment.

I also conclude for the reasons stated in the following opinion that the portion of the court's judgment enjoining petitioner from according any consideration to race in its admissions process must be reversed. For reasons expressed in separate opinions, my Brothers Mr. Justice Brennan, Mr. Justice White, Mr. Justice Marshall, and Mr. Justice Blackmun concur in this judgment.

*Affirmed in part and reversed in part.*

The Medical School of the University of California at Davis opened in 1968 with an entering class of 50 students. In 1971, the size of the entering class was increased to 100 students, a level at which it remains. No admissions program for disadvantaged or minority students existed when the school opened, and the first class contained three Asians, but no blacks, no Mexican-Americans, and no American Indians. Over the next two years, the faculty devised a special admissions program to increase the representation of "disadvantaged" students in each Medical School class. The special program consisted of a separate admissions system operating in coordination with the regular admissions process.

Under the regular admissions procedure, a candidate could submit his application to the Medical School beginning in July of the year preceding the academic year for which admission was sought. Because of the large number of applications, the admissions committee screened each one to select candidates for further consideration. Candidates whose overall undergraduate grade point averages fell below 2.5 on a scale of 4.0 were summarily rejected. About one out of six applicants was invited for a personal interview. Following the interviews, each candidate was rated on a scale of 1 to 100 by his interviewers and four other members of the admissions committee. The rating embraced the interviewers' summaries, the candidate's overall grade point average, grade point average in science courses, scores on the Medical College Admissions Test (MCAT), letters of recommendation, extracurricular activities, and other biographical data. The ratings were added together to arrive at each candidate's "benchmark" score. Since five committee members rated each candidate in 1973, a perfect score was 500; in 1974, six members rated each candidate, so that a perfect score was 600. The full committee then reviewed the files and scores of each applicant and made offers of admission on a "rolling" basis. The chairman was responsible for placing names on the waiting list. They were not placed in strict numerical order; instead, the chairman had discretion to include persons with "special skills."

The special admissions program operated with a separate committee, a majority of whom were members of minority groups. On the 1973 application form, candidates were asked to indicate whether they wished to be considered as "economically and/or educationally disadvantaged" applicants; on the 1974 form the question was whether they wished to be considered as members of a "minority group," which the Medical School apparently viewed as "Blacks," "Chicanos," "Asians," and "American Indians." If these questions were answered affirmatively, the application was forwarded to the special admissions committee. No formal definition of "disadvantaged" was ever produced, but the chairman of the special committee screened each application to see whether it reflected economic or educational deprivation. Having passed this initial hurdle, the applications then were rated by the special committee in a fashion similar to that used by the general admissions committee, except that special candidates did not have to meet the 2.5 grade point average cutoff applied to regular applicants. About one-fifth of the total number of special applicants were invited for interviews in 1973 and 1974. Following each interview, the special committee assigned each special applicant a benchmark score. The special committee then presented its top choices to the general admissions committee. The latter did not rate or compare the special candidates against the general applicants, but could reject recommended special candidates for failure to meet course requirements or other specific deficiencies. The special committee continued to recommend special applicants until a number prescribed by faculty vote were admitted. While the overall class size was still 50, the prescribed number was 8; in 1973 and 1974, when the class size had doubled to 100, the prescribed number of special admissions also doubled, to 16.

From the year of the increase in class size—1971—through 1974, the special program resulted in the admission of 21 black students, 30 Mexican-Americans, and 12 Asians, for a total of 63 minority students. Over the same period, the regular admissions program produced 1 black, 6 Mexican-Americans, and 37 Asians, for a total of 44 minority students. Although disadvantaged whites applied to the special program in large numbers, none received an offer of admission through that process. Indeed, in 1974, at least, the special committee explicitly considered only "disadvantaged" special applicants who were members of one of the designated minority groups.

Allan Bakke is a white male who applied to the Davis Medical School in both 1973 and 1974. In both years Bakke's application was considered under the general admissions program, and he received an interview. His 1973 interview was with Dr. Theodore C. West, who considered Bakke "a very desirable applicant to [the] medical school." Despite a strong benchmark score of 468 out of 500, Bakke was rejected. . . .

Although many of the Framers of the Fourteenth Amendment conceived of its primary function as bridging the vast distance between members of the Negro race and the white "majority," *Slaughter-House Cases, supra,* the Amendment itself was framed in universal terms, without reference to color, ethnic origin, or condition of prior servitude. As this Court recently remarked in interpreting the 1866 Civil Rights Act to extend to claims of racial discrimination against white persons, "the 39th Congress was intent upon establishing in the federal law a broader principle than would have been necessary simply to meet the particular and immediate plight of the newly freed Negro slaves." *McDonald v. Santa Fe Trail Transportation Co.,* 427 U.S 273, 296. And that legislation was specifically broadened in 1870 to ensure that "all persons," not merely "citizens" would enjoy equal rights under the law. . . .

Petitioner urges us to adopt for the first time a more restrictive view of the Equal Protection Clause and hold that discrimination against members of the white "majority" cannot be suspect if its purpose can be characterized as "benign." The clock of our liberties, however, cannot be turned back to 1868. . . . It is far too late to argue that the guarantee of equal protection to *all* persons permits the recognition of special wards entitled to a degree of protection greater than that accorded others. "The Fourteenth Amendment is not directed solely against discrimination due to a 'two-class theory'—that is, based upon differences between 'white' and Negro." *Hernandez,* 347 U.S., at 478.

Once the artificial line of a "two-class theory" of the Fourteenth Amendment is put aside, the difficulties entailed in varying the level of judicial review according to a perceived "preferred" status of a particular racial or ethnic minority are intractable. The concepts of "majority" and "minority" necessarily reflect temporary arrangements and political judgments. As observed above, the white "majority" itself is composed of various minority groups, most of which can lay claim to a history of prior discrimination at the hands of the State and private individuals. Not all of these groups can receive preferential treatment and corresponding judicial tolerance of distinctions drawn in terms of race and nationality, for then the only "majority" left would be a new minority of white Anglo-Saxon Protestants. There is no principled basis for deciding which groups would merit "heightened judicial solicitude" and which would not. Courts would be asked to evaluate the extent of the prejudice and consequent harm suffered by various minority groups. Those whose societal injury is thought to exceed some arbitrary level of tolerability then would be entitled to preferential classifications at the expense of individuals belonging to other groups. Those classifications would be free from exacting judicial scrutiny. As these preferences began to have their desired effect, and the consequences of past discrimination were undone, new judicial rankings would be necessary. The kind of variable sociological and political analysis necessary to produce such rankings simply does not lie within the judicial competence—even if they otherwise were politically feasible and socially desirable.

Moreover, there are serious problems of justice connected with the idea of preference itself. First, it may not always be clear that a so-called preference is in fact benign. Courts may be asked to validate burdens imposed upon individual members of a particular group in order to advance the group's general interest. See *United Jewish Organizations v. Carey*, 430 U.S., at 172–173 (Brennan, J., concurring in part). Nothing in the Constitution supports the notion that individuals may be asked to suffer otherwise impermissible burdens in order to enhance the societal standing of their ethnic groups. Second, preferential programs may only reinforce common stereotypes holding that certain groups are unable to achieve success without special protection based on a factor having no relationship to individual worth. . . . Third, there is a measure of inequity in forcing innocent persons in respondent's position to bear the burdens of redressing grievances not of their making.

By hitching the meaning of the Equal Protection Clause to these transitory considerations, we would be holding, as a constitutional principle, that judicial scrutiny of classifications touching on racial and ethnic background may vary with the ebb and flow of political forces. Disparate constitutional tolerance of such classifications well may serve to exacerbate racial and ethnic antagonisms rather than alleviate them. *United Jewish Organizations*, *supra*, 430 U.S., at 173–174 (Brennan, J., concurring in part). Also, the mutability of a constitutional principle, based upon shifting political and social judgments, undermines the chances for consistent application of the Constitution from one generation to the next, a critical feature of its coherent interpretation. *Pollock v. Farmers' Loan & Trust Co.*, 157 U.S. 429, 650–651 (1895) (White, J., dissenting). In expounding the Constitution, the Court's role is to discern "principles sufficiently absolute to give them roots throughout the community and continuity over significant periods of time, and to lift them above the level of the pragmatic political judgments of a particular time and place." A. Cox, The Role of the Supreme Court in American Government 114 (1976).

If it is the individual who is entitled to judicial protection against classifications based upon his racial or ethnic background because such distinctions impinge upon personal rights, rather than the individual only because of his membership in a particular group, then constitutional standards may be applied consistently. Political judgments regarding the necessity for the particular classification may be weighed in the constitutional balance, *Korematsu v. United States*, 323 U.S. 214 (1944), but the standard of justification will remain constant. This is as it should be, since those political judgments are the product of rough compromise struck by contending groups within the democratic process. When they touch upon an individual's race or ethnic background, he is entitled to a judicial determination that the burden he is asked to bear on that basis is precisely tailored to serve a compelling governmental interest. The Constitution guarantees that right to every person regardless of his background. . . .

The special admissions program purports to serve the purposes of: (i) "reducing the historic deficit of traditionally disfavored minorities in medical schools and in the medical profession," . . .; (ii) countering the effects of societal discrimination; (iii) increasing the number of physicians who will practice in communities currently underserved; and (iv) obtaining the educational benefits that flow from an ethnically diverse student body. It is necessary to decide which, if any, of these purposes is substantial enough to support the use of a suspect classification. . . .

We have never approved a classification that aids persons perceived as members of relatively victimized groups at the expense of other innocent individuals in the absence of judicial, legislative, or administrative findings of constitutional or statutory violations. . . . After such findings have been made, the governmental interest in preferring members of the injured groups at the expense of others is substantial, since the legal rights of the victims must be vindicated. In such a case, the extent of the injury and the consequent remedy will have been judicially, legislatively, or administratively defined. Also, the remedial action usually remains subject to continuing oversight to assure that it will work the least harm possible to other innocent persons competing for the benefit. Without such findings of constitutional or statutory violations, it cannot be said that the government has any greater interest in helping one individual than in refraining from harming another. Thus, the government has no compelling justification for inflicting such harm.

Hence, the purpose of helping certain groups whom the faculty of the Davis Medical School perceived as victims of "societal discrimination" does not justify a classification that imposes disadvantages upon persons like respondent, who bear no responsibility for whatever harm the beneficiaries of the special admissions program are thought to have suffered. To hold otherwise would be to convert a remedy heretofore reserved for violations of legal rights into a privilege that all institutions throughout the Nation could grant at their pleasure to whatever groups are perceived as victims of societal discrimination. That is a step we have never approved. . . .

Petitioner identifies, as another purpose of its program, improving the delivery of health-care services to communities currently underserved. It may be assumed that in some situations a State's interest in facilitating the health care of its citizens is sufficiently compelling to support the use of a suspect classification. But there is virtually no evidence in the record indicating that petitioner's special admissions program is either needed or geared to promote that goal. . . .

The fourth goal asserted by petitioner is the attainment of a diverse student body. This clearly is a constitutionally permissible goal for an institution of higher education. Academic freedom, though not a specifically enumerated constitutional right, long has been viewed as a special concern of the First Amendment. The freedom of a university to make its own judgments as to education includes the selection of its student body. . . .

Thus, in arguing that its universities must be accorded the right to select those students who will contribute the most to the "robust exchange of ideas," petitioner invokes a countervailing constitutional interest, that of the First Amendment. In this light, petitioner must be viewed as seeking to achieve a goal that is of paramount importance in the fulfillment of its mission. . . .

In such an admissions program, race or ethnic background may be deemed a "plus" in a particular applicant's file, yet it does not insulate the individual from comparison with all other candidates for the available seats. The file of a particular black applicant may be examined for his potential contribution to diversity without the factor of his race being decisive when compared, for example, with that of an applicant identified as an Italian-American if the latter is thought to exhibit qualities more likely to promote beneficial educational pluralism. Such qualities could include exceptional personal talents, unique work or service experience, leadership potential, maturity, demonstrated compassion, a history of overcoming disadvantage, ability to communicate with the poor, or other qualifications deemed important. In short, an admissions program operated in this way is flexible enough to consider all pertinent elements of diversity in light of the particular qualifications of each applicant, and to place them on the same footing for consideration, although not necessarily according them the same weight. Indeed, the weight attributed to a particular quality may vary from year to year depending upon the "mix" both of the student body and the applicants for the incoming class. . . .

In summary, it is evident that the Davis special admissions program involves the use of an explicit racial classification never before countenanced by this Court. It tells applicants who are not Negro, Asian, or Chicano that they are totally excluded from a specific percentage of the seats in an entering class. No matter how strong their qualifications, quantitative and extracurricular, including their own potential for contribution to educational diversity, they are never afforded the chance to compete with applicants from the preferred groups for the special admissions seats. At the same time, the preferred applicants have the opportunity to compete for every seat in the class.

The fatal flaw in petitioner's preferential program is its disregard of individual rights as guaranteed by the Fourteenth Amendment. *Shelley v. Kraemer*, 334 U.S., at 22. Such rights are not absolute. But when a State's distribution of benefits or imposition of burdens hinges on ancestry or the color of a person's skin, that individual is entitled to a demonstration that the challenged classification is necessary to promote a substantial state interest. Petitioner has failed to carry this burden. For this reason, that portion of the California court's judgment holding petitioner's special admissions program invalid under the Fourteenth Amendment must be affirmed.

## RICHMOND v. J.A. CROSON CO.
### *488 U.S. 469 (1989)*

JUSTICE O'CONNOR announced the judgment of the Court. . . .

On April 11, 1983, the Richmond City Council adopted the Minority Business Utilization Plan (the Plan). The Plan required prime contractors to whom the city awarded construction contracts to subcontract at least 30% of the dollar amount of the contract to one or more Minority Business Enterprises (MBE's). The 30% set aside did not apply to city contracts awarded to minority-owned prime contractors.

The Plan defined an MBE as "[a] business at least fifty-one (51) percent of which is owned and controlled . . . by minority group members." "Minority group members" were defined as "[c]itizens of the United States who are Blacks, Spanish-speaking, Orientals, Indians, Eskimos, or Aleuts." There was no geographic limit to the Plan; an otherwise qualified MBE from anywhere in the United States could avail itself of the 30% set-aside. The Plan declared that it was "remedial" in nature, and enacted "for the purpose of promoting wider participation by minority business enterprises in the construction of public projects." The Plan expired on June 30, 1988, and was in effect for approximately five years. . . .

The Plan was adopted by the Richmond City Council after a public hearing. Seven members of the public spoke to the merits of the ordinance: five were in opposition, two in favor. Proponents of the set-aside provision relied on a study which indicated that, while the general population of Richmond was 50% black, only 0.67% of the city's prime construction contracts had been awarded to minority businesses in the 5-year period from 1978 to 1983. It was also established that a variety of contractors' associations, whose representatives appeared in opposition to the ordinance, had virtually no minority businesses within their membership. . . .

Opponents of the ordinance questioned both its wisdom and its legality. They argued that a disparity between minorities in the population of Richmond and the number of prime contracts awarded to MBE's had little probative value in establishing discrimination in the construction industry. . . .

Councilperson Gillespie indicated his concern that many local labor jobs, held by both blacks and whites, would be lost because the ordinance put no geographic limit on the MBE's eligible for the 30% set-aside. . . .

The parties and their supporting amici fight an initial battle over the scope of the city's power to adopt legislation designed to address the effects of past discrimination. Relying on our decision in Wygant, appellee argues that the city must limit any race-based remedial efforts to eradicating the effects of its own prior discrimination. This is essentially the position taken by the Court of Appeals below. Appellant argues that our decision in Fullilove is controlling, and that as a result the city of Richmond enjoys sweeping legislative power to define and attack the effects of prior discrimination in its local construction industry. We find that neither of these two rather stark alternatives can withstand analysis.

In Fullilove, we upheld the minority set-aside contained in § 103(f)(2) of the Public Works Employment Act of 1977, Pub.L. 95–28, 91 Stat. 116, 42 U.S.C. § 6701 et seq. (Act) against a challenge based on the equal protection component of the Due Process Clause. The Act authorized a $4 billion appropriation for federal grants to state and local governments for use in public works projects. The primary purpose of the Act was to give the national economy a quick boost in a recessionary period; funds had to be committed to state or local grantees by September 30, 1977. The Act also contained the following requirement: " 'Except to the extent the Secretary determines otherwise, no grant shall be made under this Act . . . unless the applicant gives satisfactory assurance to the Secretary that at least 10 per centum of the amount of each grant shall be expended for minority business enterprises.'" *Fullilove*, 448 U.S., at 454 (quoting 91 Stat. 116, 42 U.S.C. § 6705(f)(2)). MBE's were defined as businesses effectively controlled by "citizens of the United States who are Negroes, Spanish-speaking, Orientals, Indians, Eskimos, and Aleuts."

The principal opinion in *Fullilove*, written by Chief Justice Burger, did not employ "strict scrutiny" or any other traditional standard of equal protection review. The Chief Justice noted at the outset that although racial classifications call for close examination, the Court was at the same time "bound to approach [its] task with appropriate deference to the Congress, a co-equal branch charged by the Constitution with the power to 'provide for the . . . general Welfare of the United States' and 'to enforce by appropriate legislation,' the equal protection guarantees of the Fourteenth Amendment." 448 U.S., at 472. The principal opinion asked two questions: first, were the objectives of the legislation within the power of Congress? Second, was the limited use of racial and ethnic criteria a permissible means for Congress to carry out its objectives within the constraints of the Due Process Clause? *Id.*, at 473.

On the issue of congressional power, the Chief Justice found that Congress' commerce power was sufficiently broad to allow it to reach the practices of prime contractors on federally funded local construction projects. *Id.*, at 475–476. Congress could mandate state and local government compliance with the set-aside program under its § 5 power to enforce the Fourteenth Amendment. *Id.*, at 476 100 S. Ct., at 2773 (citing *Katzenbach v. Morgan*, 374 U.S. 641, 651 (1966)).

The Chief Justice next turned to the constraints on Congress' power to employ race-conscious remedial relief. His opinion stressed two factors in upholding the MBE set-aside. First was the unique remedial powers of Congress under § 5 of the Fourteenth Amendment:

> "Here we deal . . . not with the limited remedial powers of a federal court, for example, but with the broad remedial powers of Congress. It is fundamental that *in no organ of government, state or federal, does there repose a more comprehensive remedial power than in the Congress*, expressly charged by the Constitution with competence and authority to enforce equal protection guarantees." 448 U.S., at 483 (principal opinion) (emphasis added).

Because of these unique powers, the Chief Justice concluded that "Congress not only may induce voluntary action to assure compliance with existing federal statutory or constitutional antidiscrimination provisions, but also, where Congress has authority to *declare certain conduct unlawful*, it may, as here, authorize and induce state action to avoid such conduct." *Id.*, at 483–484 (emphasis added).

In reviewing the legislative history behind the Act, the principal opinion focused on the evidence before Congress that a nationwide history of past discrimination had reduced minority participation in federal construction grants. *Id.*, at 458–467. The Chief Justice also noted that Congress drew on its experience under § 8 (a) of the Small Business Act of 1953, which had extended aid to minority businesses. *Id.*, at 463–467. The Chief Justice concluded that "Congress had abundant historical basis from which it could conclude that traditional procurement practices, when applied to minority businesses, could perpetuate the effects of prior discrimination." *Id.*, at 478.

The second factor emphasized by the principal opinion in *Fullilove* was the flexible nature of the 10% set-aside. Two "congressional assumptions" underlay the MBE program: first, that the effects of past discrimination had impaired the competitive position of minority businesses, and second, that "adjustment for the effects of past discrimination" would assure that at least 10% of the funds from the federal grant programs would flow to minority businesses. The Chief Justice noted that both of these "assumptions" could be "rebutted" by a grantee seeking a waiver of the 10% requirement. *Id.*, at 487–488. Thus a waiver could be sought where minority businesses were not available to fill the 10% requirement or, more importantly, where an MBE attempted "to exploit the remedial aspects of the program by charging an unreasonable price, *i.e.*, a price not attributable to the present effects of prior discrimination." *Id.*, at 488. The Chief Justice indicated that without this fine tuning to remedial purpose, the statute would not have "pass[ed] muster." *Id.*, at 487. . . .

What appellant ignores is that Congress, unlike any State or political subdivision, has a specific constitutional mandate to enforce the dictates of the Fourteenth Amendment. The power to "enforce" may at times also include the power to define situations which *Congress* determines threaten principles of equality and to adopt prophylactic rules to deal with those situations. See *Katzenbach v. Morgan*, 384 U.S., at 651 ("Correctly viewed, § 5 is a positive grant of legislative power authorizing Congress to exercise its discretion in determining whether and what legislation is needed to secure the guarantees of the Fourteenth Amendment"). See also *South Carolina v. Katzenbach*, 383 U.S. 301, 326 (1966) (similar interpretation of congressional power under § 2 of the Fifteenth Amendment). The Civil War Amendments themselves worked a dramatic change in the balance between congressional and state power over matters of race. Speaking of the Thirteenth and Fourteenth Amendments in *Ex parte Virginia*, 100 U.S. 339, 345 (1880), the Court stated: "They were intended to be, what they really are, limitations of the powers of the States and enlargements of the power of Congress." . . .

It would seem equally clear, however, that a state or local subdivision (if delegated the authority from the State) has the authority to eradicate the effects of private discrimination within its own legislative jurisdiction. This authority must, of course, be exercised within the constraints of § 1 of the Fourteenth Amendment. Our decision in *Wygant* is not to the contrary. *Wygant* addressed the constitutionality of the use of racial quotas by local school authorities pursuant to an agreement reached with the local teachers' union. It was in the context of addressing the school board's power to adopt a race-based layoff program affecting its own work force that the *Wygant* plurality indicated that the Equal Protection Clause required "some showing of prior discrimination by the governmental unit involved." *Wygant*, 476 U.S., at 274. As a matter of state law, the city of Richmond has legislative authority over its procurement policies, and can use its spending powers to remedy private discrimination, if it identifies that discrimination with the particularity required by the Fourteenth Amendment. To this extent, on the question of the city's competence, the Court of Appeals erred in following *Wygant* by rote in a case involving a state entity which has state-law authority to address discriminatory practices within local commerce under its jurisdiction.

Thus, if the city could show that it had essentially become a "passive participant" in a system of racial exclusion practiced by elements of the local construction industry, we think it clear that the city could take affirmative steps to dismantle such a system. It is beyond dispute that any public entity, state or federal, has a compelling interest in assuring that public dollars, drawn from the tax contributions of all citizens, do not serve to finance the evil of private prejudice. Cf. *Norwood v. Harrison*, 413 U.S. 455, 465 (1973) ("Racial discrimination in state-operated schools is barred by the Constitution and [i]t is also axiomatic that a state may not induce, encourage or promote private persons to accomplish what it is constitutionally forbidden to accomplish") (citation and internal quotations omitted).

The Equal Protection Clause of the Fourteenth Amendment provides that: "[n]o State shall . . . deny to *any person* within its jurisdiction the equal protection of the laws." (Emphasis added.) As this Court has noted in the past, the "rights created by the first section of the Fourteenth Amendment are, by its terms, guaranteed to the individual." The rights established are personal rights." *Shelley v. Kraemer*, 334 U.S. 1, 22 (1948). The Richmond Plan denies certain citizens the opportunity to compete for a fixed percentage of public contracts based solely upon their race. To whatever racial group these citizens belong, their "personal rights" to be treated with equal dignity and respect are implicated by a rigid rule erecting race as the sole criterion in an aspect of public decisionmaking.

Absent searching judicial inquiry into the justification for such race-based measures, there is simply no way of determining what classifications are "benign" or "remedial" and what classifications are in fact motivated by illegitimate notions of racial inferiority or simple racial politics. Indeed, the purpose of strict scrutiny is to "smoke out" illegitimate uses of race by assuring that the legislative body is pursuing a goal important enough to warrant use of a highly suspect tool. The test also ensures that the means chosen "fit" this compelling goal so closely that there is little or no possibility that the motive for the classification was illegitimate racial prejudice or stereotype. . . .

Our continued adherence to the standard of review employed in *Wygant* does not, as Justice Marshall's dissent suggests . . . indicate that we view "racial discrimination as largely a phenomenon of the past" or that "government bodies need no longer preoccupy themselves with rectifying racial injustice." . . . States and their local subdivisions have many legislative weapons at their disposal both to punish and prevent present discrimination and to remove arbitrary barriers to minority advancement. Rather, our interpretation of § 1 stems from our agreement with the view expressed by Justice Powell in *Bakke* that "[t]he guarantee of equal protection cannot mean one thing when applied to one individual and something else when applied to a person of another color." . . .

In *Wygant*, 476 U.S. 267 (1986), four Members of the Court applied heightened scrutiny to a race-based system of employee layoffs. Justice Powell, writing for the plurality, again drew the distinction between "societal discrimination" which is an inadequate basis for race-conscious classifications, and the type of identified discrimination that can support and define the scope of race-based relief. The challenged classification in that case tied the layoff of minority teachers to the percentage of minority students enrolled in the school district. The lower courts had upheld the scheme, based on the theory that minority students were in need of "role models" to alleviate the effects of prior discrimination in society. This Court reversed, with a plurality of four Justices reiterating the view expressed by Justice Powell in *Bakke* that

"[s]ocietal discrimination, without more, is too amorphous a basis for imposing a racially classified remedy." *Wygant, supra,* at 276.

The role model theory employed by the lower courts failed for two reasons.
First, the statistical disparity between students and teachers had no probative
value in demonstrating the kind of prior discrimination in hiring or promotion that would justify race-based relief. 476 U.S., at 276; see also *id.,* at 294
(O'Connor, J., concurring in part and concurring in judgment) ("The disparity between the percentage of minorities on the teaching staff and the
percentage of minorities in the student body is not probative of employment
discrimination"). Second, because the role model theory had no relation to
some basis for believing a constitutional or statutory violation had occurred,
it could be used to "justify" race-based decisionmaking essentially limitless in
scope and duration. *Id.,* at 276 (plurality opinion) ("In the absence of
particularized findings, a court could uphold remedies that are ageless in their
reach into the past, and timeless in their ability to affect the future").

We think it clear that the factual predicate offered in support of the
Richmond Plan suffers from the same two defects identified as fatal in
*Wygant.* The District Court found the city council's "findings sufficient to
ensure that, in adopting the Plan, it was remedying the present effects of past
discrimination in the *construction industry.*" Supp.App. 163 (emphasis added).
Like the "role model" theory employed in *Wygant,* a generalized assertion
that there has been past discrimination in an entire industry provides no
guidance for a legislative body to determine the precise scope of the injury it
seeks to remedy. It "has no logical stopping point." *Wygant, supra,* at 275
(plurality opinion). "Relief" for such an ill-defined wrong could extend until
the percentage of public contracts awarded to MBE's in Richmond mirrored
the percentage of minorities in the population as a whole.

Appellant argues that it is attempting to remedy various forms of past
discrimination that are alleged to be responsible for the small number of
minority businesses in the local contracting industry. Among these the city
cites the exclusion of blacks from skilled construction trade unions and
training programs. This past discrimination has prevented them "from following the traditional path from laborer to entrepreneur." The city also lists a
host of nonracial factors which would seem to face a member of any racial
group attempting to establish a new business enterprise, such as deficiencies
in working capital, inability to meet bonding requirements, unfamiliarity
with bidding procedures, and disability caused by an inadequate track record.

While there is no doubt that the sorry history of both private and public
discrimination in this country has contributed to a lack of opportunities for
black entrepreneurs, this observation, standing alone, cannot justify a rigid

racial quota in the awarding of public contracts in Richmond, Virginia. Like the claim that discrimination in primary and secondary schooling justifies a rigid racial preference in medical school admissions, an amorphous claim that there has been past discrimination in a particular industry cannot justify the use of an unyielding racial quota.

It is sheer speculation how many minority firms there would be in Richmond absent past societal discrimination, just as it was sheer speculation how many minority medical students would have been admitted to the medical school at Davis absent past discrimination in educational opportunities. Defining these sorts of injuries as "identified discrimination" would give local governments license to create a patchwork of racial preferences based on statistical generalizations about any particular field of endeavor. . . .

In sum, none of the evidence presented by the city points to any identified discrimination in the Richmond construction industry. We, therefore, hold that the city has failed to demonstrate a compelling interest in apportioning public contracting opportunities on the basis of race. To accept Richmond's claim that past societal discrimination alone can serve as the basis for rigid racial preferences would be to open the door to competing claims for "remedial relief" for every disadvantaged group. The dream of a Nation of equal citizens in a society where race is irrelevant to personal opportunity and achievement would be lost in a mosaic of shifting preferences based on inherently unmeasurable claims of past wrongs. "Courts would be asked to evaluate the extent of the prejudice and consequent harm suffered by various minority groups. Those whose societal injury is thought to exceed some arbitrary level of tolerability then would be entitled to preferential classifications. . . ." *Bakke*, 438 U.S., at 296–297 (Powell, J.). We think such a result would be contrary to both the letter and spirit of a constitutional provision whose central command is equality.

The foregoing analysis applies only to the inclusion of blacks within the Richmond set-aside program. There is *absolutely no evidence* of past discrimination against Spanish-speaking, Oriental, Indian, Eskimo, or Aleut persons in any aspect of the Richmond construction industry. The District Court took judicial notice of the fact that the vast majority of "minority" persons in Richmond were black. It may well be that Richmond has never had an Aleut or Eskimo citizen. The random inclusion of racial groups that, as a practical matter, may never have suffered from discrimination in the construction industry in Richmond suggests that perhaps the city's purpose was not in fact to remedy past discrimination. . . .

Nothing we say today precludes a state or local entity from taking action to rectify the effects of identified discrimination within its jurisdiction. If the city of Richmond had evidence before it that nonminority contractors were systematically excluding minority businesses from subcontracting opportunities it could take action to end the discriminatory exclusion. Where there is a significant statistical disparity between the number of qualified minority contractors willing and able to perform a particular service and the number of such contractors actually engaged by the locality or the locality's prime contractors, an inference of discriminatory exclusion could arise. See *Bazemore v. Friday*, 478 U.S., at 398; *Teamsters v. United States*, 431 U.S., at 337–339. Under such circumstances, the city could act to dismantle the closed business system by taking appropriate measures against those who discriminate on the basis of race or other illegitimate criteria. See, e.g., *New York State Club Assn. v. New York City*, 487 U.S. 1, 10–11, 13–14 (1988). In the extreme case, some form of narrowly tailored racial preference might be necessary to break down patterns of deliberate exclusions. . . .

In the case at hand, the city has not ascertained how many minority enterprises are present in the local construction market nor the level of their participation in city construction projects. The city points to no evidence that qualified minority contractors have been passed over for city contracts or subcontracts, either as a group or in any individual case. Under such circumstances, it is simply impossible to say that the city has demonstrated "a strong basis in evidence for its conclusion that remedial action was necessary." *Wygant*, 476 U.S., at 277.

.................................DISCUSSION QUESTIONS.............................

1. The justices who have been critical of affirmative action plans have made several arguments. Justice Scalia has argued that, when making decisions about admission and hiring, public universities and government employers should be allowed to take into account the kind of economic and social environment in which applicants have grown up. In a very real sense, he is arguing for affirmative action for the poor. He argues that since many of the economically disadvantaged in the United States are also minorities, this kind of affirmative action plan would have a significant impact on minorities without carrying the stigma that affirmative action plans based strictly on race carry. What do you think of his argument? If Justice Thomas, who is black, made the same argument, would it carry more weight with you?

2. Justice O'Connor has criticized simplistic affirmative action plans that only look at the number of minorities in the general labor pool without

considering how many minorities are qualified for a particular type of job or have any interest in obtaining a particular type of job. What do you think of this criticism? Since the U.S. Labor Department is probably the only government agency capable of providing real information in this regard, do you think it should try to come up with answers to these questions?

3. Justice Stevens has argued that the goal of providing role models for minorities justifies affirmative action plans for filling certain job openings such as those for police and teachers. What other jobs do you think would qualify? Should it make any difference if the minority person who receives special treatment from such an affirmative action plan has just arrived in the United States and has never suffered any past discrimination in this country?

4. A key issue in the twenty-first century may be deciding when to bring affirmative action plans to an end. What factors should be taken into account in making this kind of decision?

5. President Johnson signed Executive Order 11246, which requires companies that contract with the federal government to implement affirmative action plans. This has been the major affirmative action program of the federal government since the 1960s. Presidents Reagan and Bush talked a lot about their dislike for affirmative action plans, but they never rescinded this executive order, something they could have done with the stroke of a pen. Why do you think they never did this?

# CHAPTER
## five
·❋·❋·❋·❋·❋·

# Congress and Racial Integration

·············································· **DISCUSSION** ··········································

After the Thirteenth Amendment was ratified, Congress passed the Civil Rights Act of 1865. This act was passed to protect the right of "all citizens," including minorities, to do such things as "make and enforce contracts" and "buy, sell, inherit, and lease property." President Andrew Johnson vetoed the act because in his opinion the Thirteenth Amendment did not give the federal government the power to prohibit racial discrimination in the states. Congress overrode his veto, but members of Congress began to wonder whether the Thirteenth Amendment really did give them the authority to pass civil rights laws. Because of these doubts, Congress passed the Fourteenth Amendment, which was then ratified by the states. Ultimately, the Fifteenth Amendment was passed to address doubts over the power of the Fourteenth Amendment to control voting. The original civil rights act was repassed along with other provisions in a series of civil rights acts passed in 1870, 1871, and 1875.

The Civil Rights Act of 1875 was designed to protect the right of all citizens to enjoy public accommodations. It stated:

> All persons within the jurisdiction of the United States shall be entitled to the full and equal enjoyment of the accommodations, advantages, facilities, and privileges of inns, public conveyances on land or water, theatres, and other places of public amusement; subject only to the conditions and limitations established by law, and applicable alike to citizens of every race and color, regardless of any previous condition of servitude.

The act allowed people who had been denied the "full and equal enjoyment" of public accommodations to sue in federal court and provided for criminal penalties for violations of the act.

## THE CIVIL RIGHTS CASES OF 1883

In 1883 five different appeals concerning the constitutionality of the Civil Rights Act of 1875 arrived at the Supreme Court and were consolidated into what the Court simply called the *Civil Rights Cases* (see p. 92). These cases involved private business owners who did not want to serve black people, or who did not want to serve black people in the same area or in the same way they served white people. These private business people were then prosecuted under the Civil Rights Act of 1875 for racial discrimination. The only issue in these cases was whether Congress had the power to pass a civil rights law of this kind, because if the law was declared unconstitutional the prosecutions would be overturned.

Justice Bradley, in writing the majority opinion, looked first to the Fourteenth Amendment. Although Congress had passed the Fourteenth Amendment thinking it would provide the broad powers Congress needed to deal with the issue of racial integration, the amendment says very specifically that it applies only to the actions of states. The amendment says "[n]o State shall make or enforce any law" which shall deny equal protection. No state law was involved in the *Civil Rights Cases*. Justice Bradley found:

> [C]ivil rights, such as are guaranteed by the constitution against state aggression, cannot be impaired by the wrongful acts of individuals, unsupported by state authority in the shape of laws, customs, or judicial or executive proceedings. The wrongful act of an individual, unsupported by any such authority, is simply a private wrong. . . .

He did not believe the Fourteenth Amendment gave Congress the authority to outlaw this kind of private wrong. The Fourteenth Amendment only outlawed wrongs committed by state and local governments.

Justice Bradley then turned to the Thirteenth Amendment. The Thirteenth Amendment simply says that "slavery" and "involuntary servitude" shall no longer exist. But there was no slavery or involuntary servitude in these cases, simply private discrimination based on race by private businesses. Those who argued in favor of congressional power to address private wrongs argued that, by extension, the Thirteenth Amendment gave Congress the power to abolish "all badges" of slavery and that this included the power to outlaw racial segregation by private businesses engaged in public accommodation. Justice Bradley rejected this idea. He did not agree that the act of "a mere individual" could be seen to impose a badge of slavery or servitude. The Civil Rights Act of 1875 was declared unconstitutional.

Only Justice Harlan dissented from this opinion. He believed that the "substance and spirit" of the Thirteenth and Fourteenth Amendments had been "sacrificed by a subtle and ingenious verbal criticism." In his view, the idea that the Thirteenth Amendment gave Congress the power to eradicate the "badges and incidents" of slavery should be "indisputable."

With the decision in the *Civil Rights Cases* in 1883, much of the federal government's efforts to bring about racial integration after the Civil War came to an end. Some of the civil rights provisions were repealed; others were simply forgotten. Several provisions, however, remained in the federal statute books.

- Title 42 Section 1981 provided that everyone should have the right to "make and enforce contracts, to sue, be parties, give evidence, and to the full and equal benefit of all laws."
- Title 42 Section 1982 provided that all citizens should have the same right "as is enjoyed by white citizens" to "inherit, purchase, lease, sell, hold, and convey real and personal property."
- Title 42 Section 1983 allowed people who had been deprived of their civil rights "under color of any statute, regulation, custom, or usage, of any State or Territory or the District of Columbia" to sue for damages.
- Title 42 Section 1985(3) allowed for a suit against any group of "two or more persons" who conspired to deprive someone of the "equal protection of the laws, or of equal privileges and immunities under the law."
- Title 18 Section 241 provided criminal penalties if two or more persons conspired to "injure, oppress, threaten, or intimidate any inhabitant of any State, Territory or District in the free exercise or enjoyment of any right or privilege secured" by the Constitution or the laws of the United States.
- Title 18 Section 242 provided criminal penalties for anyone who "under color of any law, statute, ordinance, regulation, or custom" willfully subjected anyone to the "deprivation of any rights, privileges, or immunities secured or protected" by the Constitution or laws of the United States.

Between the 1880s and the 1960s, the Supreme Court became more willing to allow Congress to act to prevent racial discrimination if the action could in any way be seen to fall under the congressional power to regulate "interstate commerce." The Court was also willing to act without further guidance from Congress to protect the right of black citizens to vote. In addition, during this period, the Court expanded its ideas of what constituted "state action" in order to end some kinds of racial discrimination.

## THE WHITE PRIMARY CASES

During the first half of the twentieth century, the Supreme Court handed down a series of decisions about the right of black citizens to vote. After the Civil War, southern states had developed an election system in which the Democratic Party primary election was the important election because the Democratic candidate always won the general election. The states then excluded black people from voting in the primary election, which meant that blacks were excluded from voting in the election that counted. In the 1927 case of *Nixon v. Herndon*, L. A. Nixon, a black man, sued the election judges for refusing to allow him to vote in the Texas Democratic Party primary. A Texas statute stated that "in no event shall a Negro be eligible to participate in a Democratic party election held in the State of Texas."

Justice Holmes wrote the opinion for the unanimous Court. In a very short opinion, he held that the statute clearly violated the Fourteenth Amendment's Equal Protection Clause. A state could not pass laws that prevented black people from voting in a Democratic Party primary election.

Texas replaced this statute with one that gave the state executive committee of each political party the power to "prescribe the qualifications" of the party's own members and to decide who would be allowed to vote in its primary election. The state executive committee of the Texas Democratic Party then passed a rule that prevented black people from voting in the Democratic Party primary election. L. A. Nixon was again denied the right to vote in the Democratic Party primary, and once again he sued. In the 1932 case of *Nixon v. Condon,* the Court again decided in Nixon's favor with a vote of five to four.

The Democratic Party argued that it was a private organization, and, therefore, the Court did not have the power to force the party to change its procedure. Justice Cardozo, writing for the majority, rejected this idea, finding that the new law delegated the state's power to decide who could vote in the primary to the Democratic Party's executive committee, and therefore that committee was acting as an agent of the state.

After this decision, the state convention of the Texas Democratic Party passed a rule barring blacks from the party primary. In the 1935 case of *Grovey v. Townsend*, a unanimous Court allowed this rule to stand. Because there was no "state action," this was viewed as simply a decision by a group of private citizens and beyond the reach of the Thirteenth, Fourteenth, or Fifteenth Amendments.

There was a significant change in the membership of the Court during the next few years, and the New Deal Court overturned the *Grovey* decision with the decision of *Smith v. Allwright* in 1944. Justice Reed, writing for the seven-justice majority, ruled that, where a state has essentially turned over control of an important part of the election process to a political party, the action of that political party can be considered to be the same as action by the state. While the earlier cases had been concerned primarily with the reach of the Fourteenth Amendment, the *Smith v. Allwright* decision rested primarily on the Fifteenth Amendment.

While these decisions and others helped to bring an end to the "white primaries" in the South, they did not result in a significant increase in black voters. Many southern states proved to be very adept at creating and using a wide variety of mechanisms, including intimidation, to prevent blacks from voting. The Supreme Court proved to be virtually powerless, acting alone, to bring an end to this fact of life in the South.

## THE QUESTION OF STATE ACTION

Beginning in the 1940s, a Supreme Court whose members were becoming more and more receptive to the idea of expanding civil rights for black citizens handed down decisions that expanded the scope of "state action" and therefore expanded the reach of civil rights laws and the Fourteenth Amendment.

In the 1948 case of *Shelley v. Kraemer*, the Court was faced with cases from Missouri and Michigan involving racially restrictive covenants. These covenants were agreements that property owners signed stating that they would not sell their property to "people of the Negro or Mongolian race." When, decades later, some of the property owners sold property to blacks, the other property owners sued to keep the black buyers from occupying the property. State courts in Missouri and Michigan issued orders to enforce the covenants and prevent the black people from living on the land they had purchased.

Justice Vinson wrote the opinion for the six-justice majority. He began with the assumption that the Fourteenth Amendment would protect blacks from any *state* action that would interfere with their right to "acquire, enjoy, own and dispose of property." The restrictive covenants were clearly the action of private individuals and did not amount to state action. The orders issued by the state courts to enforce the racially discriminatory covenants, however, were clearly a racially discriminatory state action, which was forbidden by the Fourteenth Amendment. In other words, while people could place racially discriminatory restrictive covenants on property, they could not use the power of the state to enforce the covenants. No justices dissented, but Justices Reed, Jackson, and Rutledge did not take part in the decision.

The 1961 case of *Burton v. Wilmington Parking Authority* involved the Eagle Coffee Shoppe, which was located inside a government-owned parking building in Wilmington, Delaware. The Eagle Coffee Shoppe refused to serve William Burton simply because he was black. The Delaware Supreme Court concluded that the Eagle Coffee Shoppe was a restaurant, not an inn, under Delaware law and was therefore not required to serve all comers. The state supreme court also concluded that the racial discrimination in this case was private discrimination and so did not violate the Fourteenth Amendment or federal civil rights laws.

Justice Clark, writing for the six-justice majority, came to a very different conclusion. He found that this action was the equivalent of "state action." The parking garage was owned by a government agency, the Wilmington Parking Authority, which in turn leased space to the Eagle Coffee Shoppe. The authority could have required the shop, as its tenant, not to discriminate. Justice Clark also pointed out that the land and building were owned by the government and that the restaurant was an "integral part" of a public building. When a state or local government leases property, he concluded, it must make sure that the lessee abides by the requirements of the Fourteenth Amendment "as certainly as though they were binding covenants written into the agreement."

Justices Harlan, Whittaker, and Frankfurter dissented. They argued that the case should be sent back for further proceedings before the Supreme Court decided the case.

While these and other decisions demonstrated the willingness of the Supreme Court to stretch a point in its efforts to help bring an end to racial discrimination, they were not very effective in bringing an end to private racial segregation in American society. In reality, the state action doctrine could only be stretched so far. It became clear that congressional action would be needed.

## THE CIVIL RIGHTS ACT OF 1964

In the 1960s an unprecedented alignment occurred among the three branches of the federal government. For the first time in American history, the Supreme Court, the president, and a majority of the members of Congress were ready to take significant action to end racial segregation and extend full civil rights to black Americans. After a great deal of political conflict, the Civil Rights Act of 1964 was passed.

While this act contained many provisions, the two provisions with the greatest impact addressed discrimination in public accommodations and in private employment. The act outlawed discrimination in places of public accommodation such as restaurants and inns. Congress had tried to outlaw this discrimination with the Civil Rights Act of 1875, which was declared unconstitutional by the Supreme Court in the *Civil Rights Cases*. The provision on employment discrimination, Title VII, stated:

(a) It shall be unlawful employment for an employer:

    (1) to fail or refuse to hire or to discharge any individual, or otherwise to discriminate against any individual with respect to his compensation, terms, conditions, or privileges of employment, because of such individual's race, color, religion, sex, or national origin, or

    (2) to limit, segregate, or classify his employees or applicants for employment in any way which would deprive or tend to deprive any individual of employment opportunities or otherwise adversely affect his status as an employee because of such individual's race, color, religion, sex, or national origin (42 U.S.C. sec. 2000e-2).

Congress, aware of the fate of the 1875 Civil Rights Act, declared that these provisions were passed under its authority to control interstate commerce. While the act only affected businesses that had something to do with interstate commerce, this included almost all businesses, because most businesses used or made products that flowed in interstate commerce or used a means of interstate commerce such as a telephone. During the twentieth century the Supreme Court had been willing to allow Congress great latitude in passing laws related to interstate commerce, and the Court upheld this civil rights act as a reasonable use of federal power.

The 1964 Civil Rights Act also created the Equal Employment Opportunity Commission (EEOC) to write interpretative regulations and help enforce the provisions of the act as far as employment discrimination was concerned.

## REDISCOVERING THE THIRTEENTH AMENDMENT

Even with the passage of the 1964 Civil Rights Act, a great deal of private discrimination still was not prohibited by federal law. Finally, in 1968, the Court was ready to reexamine the reach of the Thirteenth Amendment. In *Jones v. Alfred H. Mayer Co.* (see p. 100), the Court was faced with a case that could not in any way be considered state action and that did not have anything to do with interstate commerce. The Alfred H. Mayer Co., a land developer, refused to sell any of the houses in its development to blacks. All the facilities in the development, such as the sewers and sidewalks, were privately owned. The issue was whether or not any federal law prohibited this private racially motivated discrimination, and, if it did, what gave Congress the authority to pass such a law.

Justice Stewart, writing for the seven-member majority, ruled that Section 1982 of the 1866 Civil Rights Act, which states that all citizens should have the same right "as is enjoyed by white citizens" to "inherit, purchase, lease, sell, hold, and convey real and personal property" outlawed this kind of private discrimination. He then concluded that the Thirteenth Amendment gave Congress the authority to prohibit private racial discrimination. Of course, this argument had been rejected by the Court in 1883 in the *Civil Rights Cases*, so the basic principle of that decision was now overturned. Justice Stewart went on to say that if Congress did not have the authority to ensure minorities at least the "freedom to buy whatever a white man can buy" and "the right to live wherever a white man can live" then the promise of the Thirteenth Amendment would be a " 'mere paper guarantee.' "

Justices Harlan and White dissented. They did not think that Section 1982 could be interpreted to reach "purely private" actions. They also did not believe the Thirteenth Amendment gave Congress the power to reach private actions.

In the 1969 case of *Sullivan v. Little Hunting Park, Inc.*, the Court extended this interpretation of Section 1982 of the 1866 Civil Rights Act to allow people to sue for damages. The case involved Paul Sullivan, who rented his house in Fairfax County, Virginia, to a black man, T. R. Freeman. The subdivision owned several recreational facilities, and the Little Hunting Park company was a private company formed to maintain those facilities. When Paul Sullivan tried to transfer the right to use those facilities to T. R. Freeman, the company refused to allow this. Justice Douglas, writing for the six-justice majority, ruled that the company could not refuse to allow Paul Sullivan to assign his right to use the facilities to T. R. Freeman.

Justice Harlan dissented, joined by Chief Justice Burger and Justice White. Justice Harlan thought that because the old civil rights laws had been first forgotten and then followed by the 1968 Fair Housing Act, the Court should limit itself to the provisions of the new law rather than expanding the reach of the old and essentially long-forgotten law.

In 1976 the Court breathed new life into Section 1981 of Title 42 of the 1866 Civil Rights Act, which provides that everyone should have the same right to "make and enforce contracts." In *Runyan v. McCrary* Justice Stewart wrote the majority opinion. The case involved Bobbe's Private School in Arlington, Virginia, and Fairfax-Brewster School in Fairfax County, Virginia. Both of these private schools refused to admit students who were not white. The Gonzales family received advertisements addressed to "resident" from both schools, but, when they tried to enroll their son Colin, they were turned away first by the Fairfax-Brewster School and then by the Bobbe's School. When Mrs. McCrary, who was black, tried to enroll her son, Michael McCrary, in Bobbe's School, she was told that only white children were accepted.

Justice Stewart, writing for the majority, ruled that Section 1981 prohibits racial discrimination by private, nonsectarian schools because Section 1981 prohibits racial discrimination in the making and enforcement of private contracts. The Gonzaleses and the McCrarys had a right to make a "private contract" free from racial discrimination, and that right had been violated.

Justice White dissented, joined by Justice Rehnquist. Justice White argued that Section 1981 should be interpreted to reach state action but not private action.

## THE FIFTEENTH AMENDMENT AND VOTING RIGHTS LAWS

In 1870 Congress passed laws making it a criminal offense for either public officials or private persons to obstruct the right to vote. In 1871 Congress required federal supervision of voter registration and federal certification of election returns. By the end of the 1870s, these laws were considered part of Reconstruction and were no longer enforced. In 1894 most of the federal voting rights laws were repealed. While the Supreme Court tried in the first half of the twentieth century to ensure the right of blacks to vote, that proved impossible. Finally, in 1965, Congress passed the Voting Rights Act (Title 42 Section 1973). The act was a response to various tests that were used in the South to justify denying the right to vote to blacks.

Because many blacks in the South were uneducated, literacy tests, which required people to prove they had the ability to read and write, kept many blacks from registering to vote. Other tests, such as tests of "good character" and tests to see whether people could understand and interpret complex legal documents, kept most blacks from voting. In 1959 a unanimous Supreme Court had refused to strike down the use of literacy tests in *Lassiter v. Northampton Election Board*. The Court reasoned that literacy was race neutral. There was good reason to believe, however, that these literacy tests were not administered to whites in the same way they were administered to blacks.

With the passage of the 1965 Voting Rights Act, tests such as literacy tests became illegal in states that Congress believed had used the tests to discriminate against blacks. In 1966, in the case of *South Carolina v. Katzenbach*, the Supreme Court found the Voting Rights Act to be constitutional under the Fifteenth Amendment. Chief Justice Warren wrote the opinion for the unanimous Court. The chief justice pointed out that, despite the efforts of the Supreme Court and Congress, the registration of voting-age blacks in Mississippi only rose from 4.9 to 6.4 percent from 1954 to 1964. Chief Justice Warren thought that it was reasonable for Congress to conclude that "sterner and more elaborate measures" were needed to end racial discrimination in voting.

The Voting Rights Act allowed the U.S. attorney general (who was Nicholas Katzenbach at the time) to review voting practices and determine which states, counties, and political subdivisions were discriminating against nonwhite voters. Using rules set out in the act, the attorney general could identify those places that had a "test or device" that limited voter registration as well as those places in which less than 50 percent of the voting-age residents were registered to vote in the 1964 presidential election. The act also allowed the attorney general to appoint voting examiners to go into these states, counties, or political subdivisions (which were mainly in the South) and register voters who met all requirements for registration other than the illegal test. The act also required that any changes in voting requirements in the areas that were affected by the act had to be approved by the attorney general. Chief Justice Warren found this to be within the power of Congress as well.

In 1970 the Voting Rights Act was amended. The Supreme Court reviewed the constitutionality of the act in the 1970 decision of *Oregon v. Mitchell*. As different sections of the act were being considered, the Court divided into different voting blocks. A unanimous Court ruled that Congress had the power to end literacy tests across the country. With a vote of eight to one, the Court accepted the idea that Congress could establish uniform standards for voter registration and absentee balloting. By a vote of five to four, the Court upheld the power of Congress to lower the voting age to 18 in all federal elections. By a vote of five to four, however, the Court ruled that Congress did not have the power under the Fifteenth Amendment to lower the voting age to 18 for state and local elections.

In 1964 the Twenty-fourth Amendment was ratified, which outlawed the use of poll taxes or other taxes that limited the right to vote, and in 1971 the Twenty-sixth Amendment was ratified, which made the national voting age

18, overturning that part of the decision in *Oregon v. Mitchell* that had found this action beyond the power of Congress.

Since 1970 the federal voting rights laws have been amended and extended several times. Black voter registration in the South increased steadily during the 1970s and 1980s as a direct result.

## CONCLUSION

Immediately following the ratification of the Thirteenth, Fourteenth, and Fifteenth Amendments, the Supreme Court interpreted these amendments in a very limited way. Much of the civil rights legislation passed soon after the Civil War was declared to be unconstitutional. A century passed before the Court again confronted the issue of what power these amendments gave Congress to overcome racial discrimination.

In the 1960s the Court overturned the decisions handed down soon after the Civil War and interpreted these three amendments in an expansive way, allowing Congress great power to overcome racial discrimination. The Court also reinterpreted civil rights laws that had been passed soon after the Civil War and were still on the federal statute books, giving the federal government more power to overcome racial discrimination by both governments and private individuals. This new interpretation, combined with new civil rights laws, brought about an amazing change in American society.

The areas where Congress and the Supreme Court have been in greatest agreement, voting and public accommodation, have brought millions of black Americans into the political process and have brought an end to the "for whites only" signs across the South. If someone had gone to sleep in 1964 and awakened in 1994, he or she would be astounded by the changes. The idea that a black person would someday be governor of Virginia or speaker of the house in North Carolina would have been unthinkable in the early 1960s. Both were realities by the early 1990s.

## CASE DECISIONS

In 1883, with a decision in the *Civil Rights Cases*, a majority of justices declared the Civil Rights Act of 1875 to be unconstitutional. This decision brought an end to much of the federal enforcement of civil rights. Justice Bradley wrote the majority opinion, which is included here. Justice Harlan, the only dissenting justice, wrote a dissenting opinion, which is also included.

In the 1968, seven-to-two decision of *Jones v. Alfred H. Mayer Co.*, the Court breathed new life into civil rights laws that had been passed after the Civil War and then forgotten. Justice Stewart wrote the majority opinion, which is included here. Justice Douglas wrote a concurring opinion and Justice Harlan wrote a dissenting opinion; these two opinions are not included.

Following are excerpts from the case decisions.

❋ ❋ ❋ ❋ ❋ ❋ ❋ ❋ ❋

## CIVIL RIGHTS CASES
### *109 U.S. 3 (1883)*

BRADLEY, J., delivered the opinion of the Court.

These cases are all founded on the first and second sections of the act of congress known as the "Civil Rights Act," passed March 1, 1875, entitled "An act to protect all citizens in their civil and legal rights." 18 St. 335. Two of the cases, those against Stanley and Nichols, are indictments for denying to persons of color the accommodations and privileges of an inn or hotel; two of them, those against Ryan and Singleton, are, one an information, the other an indictment, for denying to individuals the privileges and accommodations of a theater, the information against Ryan being for refusing a colored person a seat in the dress circle of Maguire's theater in San Francisco; and the indictment against Singleton being for denying to another person, whose color is not stated, the full enjoyment of the accommodations of the theater known as the Grand Opera House in New York, "said denial not being made for any reasons by law applicable to citizens of every race and color, and regardless of any previous condition of servitude." . . .

It is obvious that the primary and important question in all the cases is the constitutionality of the law; for if the law is unconstitutional none of the prosecutions can stand.

The sections of the law referred to provide as follows:

> "Section 1. That all persons within the jurisdiction of the United States shall be entitled to the full and equal enjoyment of the accommodations, advantages, facilities, and privileges of inns, public conveyances on land or water, theaters, and other places of public amusement; subject only to the conditions and limitations established by law, and applicable alike to citizens of every race and color, regardless of any previous condition of servitude.

"Sec. 2. That any person who shall violate the foregoing section by denying to any citizen, except for reasons by law applicable to citizens of every race and color, and regardless of any previous condition of servitude, the full enjoyment of any of the accommodations, advantages, facilities, or privileges in said section enumerated, or by aiding or inciting such denial, shall, for every such offense, forfeit and pay the sum of $500 to the person aggrieved thereby, to be recovered in an action of debt, with full costs; and shall, also, for every such offense, be deemed guilty of a misdemeanor, and upon conviction thereof shall be fined not less than $500 nor more than $1,000, or shall be imprisoned not less than 30 days nor more than one year: Provided, that all persons may elect to sue for the penalty aforesaid, or to proceed under their rights at common law and by state statutes; and having so elected to proceed in the one mode or the other, their right to proceed in the other jurisdiction shall be barred. But this provision shall not apply to criminal proceedings, either under this act or the criminal law of any state: And provided, further, that a judgment for the penalty in favor of the party aggrieved, or a judgment upon an indictment, shall be a bar to either prosecution respectively."

Are these sections constitutional? The first section, which is the principal one, cannot be fairly understood without attending to the last clause, which qualifies the preceding part.

The essence of the law is, not to declare broadly that all persons shall be entitled to the full and equal enjoyment of the accommodations, advantages, facilities, and privileges of inns, public conveyances, and theaters; but that such enjoyment shall not be subject to any conditions applicable only to citizens of a particular race or color, or who had been in a previous condition of servitude. In other words, it is the purpose of the law to declare that, in the enjoyment of the accommodations and privileges of inns, theaters, and other places of public amusement, no distinction shall be made between citizens of different race or color, or between those who have, and those who have not, been slaves. Its effect is to declare that in all inns, public conveyances, and places of amusement, colored citizens, whether formerly slaves or not, and citizens of other races, shall have the same accommodations and privileges in all inns, public conveyances, and places of amusement, as are enjoyed by white citizens; and *vice versa*. The second section makes it a penal offense in any person to deny to any citizen of any race or color, regardless of previous servitude, any of the accommodations or privileges mentioned in the first section.

Has congress constitutional power to make such a law? Of course, no one will contend that the power to pass it was contained in the constitution before the adoption of the last three amendments. The power is sought, first, in the fourteenth amendment, and the views and arguments of distinguished senators, advanced while the law was still under consideration, claiming authority to pass it by virtue of that amendment, are the principal arguments adduced in favor of the power. We have carefully considered those arguments, as was due to the eminent ability of those who put them forward, and have felt, in all its force, the weight of authority which always invests a law that congress deems itself competent to pass. But the responsibility of an independent judgment is now thrown upon this court; and we are bound to exercise it according to the best lights we have.

The first section of the fourteenth amendment,—which is the one relied on,—after declaring who shall be citizens of the United States, and of the several states, is prohibitory in its character, and prohibitory upon the states. It declares that "no state shall make or enforce any law which shall abridge the privileges or immunities of citizens of the United States; nor shall any state deprive any person of life, liberty, or property without due process of law; nor deny to any person within its jurisdiction the equal protection of the laws." It is state action of a particular character that is prohibited. Individual invasion of individual rights is not the subject-matter of the amendment. It has a deeper and broader scope. It nullifies and makes void all state legislation, and state action of every kind, which impairs the privileges and immunities of citizens of the United States, or which injures them in life, liberty, or property without due process of law, or which denies to any of them the equal protection of the laws. It not only does this, but, in order that the national will, thus declared, may not be a mere *brutum fulmen*, the last section of the amendment invests congress with power to enforce it by appropriate legislation. To enforce what? To enforce the prohibition. To adopt appropriate legislation for correcting the effects of such prohibited state law and state acts, and thus to render them effectually null, void, and innocuous. This is the legislative power conferred upon congress, and this is the whole of it. It does not invest congress with power to legislate upon subjects which are within the domain of state legislation; but to provide modes of relief against state legislation, or state action, of the kind referred to. It does not authorize congress to create a code of municipal law for the regulation of private rights; but to provide modes of redress against the operation of state laws, and the action of state officers, executive or judicial, when these are subversive of the fundamental rights specified in the amendment. Positive rights and privileges are undoubtedly secured by the fourteenth amendment; but they are secured by way of prohibition against state laws and state proceedings affecting these rights and privileges, and by power given to congress to legislate for the purpose of carrying such prohibition into effect; and such legislation must necessarily be predicated upon such supposed state laws or state proceedings, and be directed to the correction of their operation and effect. . . .

In this connection it is proper to state that civil rights, such as are guarantied by the constitution against state aggression, cannot be impaired by the wrongful acts of individuals, unsupported by state authority in the shape of laws, customs, or judicial or executive proceedings. The wrongful act of an individual, unsupported by any such authority, is simply a private wrong, or a crime of that individual; an invasion of the rights of the injured party, it is true, whether they affect his person, his property, or his reputation; but if not sanctioned in some way by the state, or not done under state authority, his rights remain in full force, and may presumably be vindicated by resort to the laws of the state for redress. An individual cannot deprive a man of his right to vote, to hold property, to buy and to sell, to sue in the courts, or to be a witness or a juror; he may, by force or fraud, interfere with the enjoyment of the right in a particular case; he may commit an assault against the person, or commit murder, or use ruffian violence at the polls, or slander the good name of a fellow-citizen; but unless protected in these wrongful acts by some shield of state law or state authority, he cannot destroy or injure the right; he will only render himself amenable to satisfaction or punishment; and amenable therefor to the laws of the state where the wrongful acts are committed. Hence, in all those cases where the constitution seeks to protect the rights of citizens against discriminative and unjust laws of the state by prohibiting such laws, it is not individual offenses, but abrogation and denial of rights, which it denounces, and for which it clothes the congress with power to provide a remedy. This abrogation and denial of rights, for which the states alone were or could be responsible, was the great seminal and fundamental wrong which was intended to be remedied. And the remedy to be provided must necessarily be predicated upon that wrong. It must assume that in the cases provided for, the evil or wrong actually committed rests upon some state law or state authority for its excuse and perpetration. . . .

But the power of congress to adopt direct and primary, as distinguished from corrective, legislation on the subject at hand, is sought, in the second place from the thirteenth amendment, which abolishes slavery. This amendment declares "that neither slavery, nor involuntary servitude, except as a punishment for crime, whereof the party shall have been duly convicted, shall exist within the United States, or any place subject to their jurisdiction;" and it gives congress power to enforce the amendment by appropriate legislation.

This amendment, as well as the fourteenth, is undoubtedly self-executing without any ancillary legislation, so far as its terms are applicable to any existing state of circumstances. By its own unaided force and effect it abolished slavery, and established universal freedom. Still, legislation may be necessary and proper to meet all the various cases and circumstances to be affected by it, and to prescribe proper modes of redress for its violation in letter or spirit. And such legislation may be primary and direct in its character; for the amendment is not a mere prohibition of state laws establishing or upholding slavery, but an absolute declaration that slavery or involuntary servitude shall not exist in any part of the United States.

It is true that slavery cannot exist without law any more than property in lands and goods can exist without law, and therefore the thirteenth amendment may be regarded as nullifying all state laws which establish or uphold slavery. But it has a reflex character also, establishing and decreeing universal civil and political freedom throughout the United States; and it is assumed that the power vested in congress to enforce the article by appropriate legislation, clothes congress with power to pass all laws necessary and proper for abolishing all badges and incidents of slavery in the United States; and upon this assumption it is claimed that this is sufficient authority for declaring by law that all persons shall have equal accommodations and privileges in all inns, public conveyances, and places of public amusement; the argument being that the denial of such equal accommodations and privileges is in itself a subjection to a species of servitude within the meaning of the amendment. Conceding the major proposition to be true, that congress has a right to enact all necessary and proper laws for the obliteration and prevention of slavery, with all its badges and incidents, is the minor proposition also true, that the denial to any person of admission to the accommodations and privileges of an inn, a public conveyance, or a theater, does subject that person to any form of servitude, or tend to fasten upon him any badge of slavery? If it does not, then power to pass the law is not found in the thirteenth amendment.

In a very able and learned presentation of the cognate question as to the extent of the rights, privileges, and immunities of citizens which cannot rightfully be abridged by state laws under the fourteenth amendment, made in a former case, a long list of burdens and disabilities of a servile character, incident to feudal vassalage in France, and which were abolished by the decrees of the national assembly, was presented for the purpose of showing that all inequalities and observances exacted by one man from another, were servitudes or badges of slavery, which a great nation, in its efforts to establish universal liberty, made haste to wipe out and destroy. But these were servitudes imposed by the old law, or by long custom which had the force of law, and exacted by one man from another without the latter's consent. Should any such servitudes be imposed by a state law, there can be no doubt that the law would be repugnant to the fourteenth, no less than to the thirteenth, amendment; nor any greater doubt that congress has adequate power to forbid any such servitude from being exacted.

But is there any similarity between such servitudes and a denial by the owner of an inn, a public conveyance, or a theater, of its accommodations and privileges to an individual, even though the denial be founded on the race or color of that individual? Where does any slavery or servitude, or badge of either, arise from such an act of denial? Whether it might not be a denial of a right which, if sanctioned by the state law, would be obnoxious to the prohibitions of the fourteenth amendment, is another question. But what has it to do with the question of slavery? . . .

Now, conceding, for the sake of the argument, that the admission to an inn, a public conveyance, or a place of public amusement, on equal terms with all other citizens, is the right of every man and all classes of men, is it any more than one of those rights which the states by the fourteenth amendment are forbidden to deny to any person? and is the constitution violated until the denial of the right has some state sanction or authority? Can the act of a mere individual, the owner of the inn, the public conveyance, or place of amusement, refusing the accommodation, be justly regarded as imposing any badge of slavery or servitude upon the applicant, or only as inflicting an ordinary civil injury, properly cognizable by the laws of the state, and presumably subject to redress by those laws until the contrary appears?

After giving to these questions all the consideration which their importance demands, we are forced to the conclusion that such an act of refusal has nothing to do with slavery or involuntary servitude, and that if it is violative of any right of the party, his redress is to be sought under the laws of the state; or, if those laws are adverse to his rights and do not protect him, his remedy will be found in the corrective legislation which congress has adopted, or may adopt, for counteracting the effect of state laws, or state action, prohibited by the fourteenth amendment. It would be running the slavery argument into the ground to make it apply to every act of discrimination which a person may see fit to make as to the guests he will entertain, or as to the people he will take into his coach or cab or car, or admit to his concert or theater, or deal with in other matters of intercourse or business. Innkeepers and public carriers, by the laws of all the states, so far as we are aware, are bound, to the extent of their facilities, to furnish proper accommodation to all unobjectionable persons who in good faith apply for them. If the laws themselves make any unjust discrimination, amenable to the prohibitions of the fourteenth amendment, congress has full power to afford a remedy under that amendment and in accordance with it.

When a man has emerged from slavery, and by the aid of beneficent legislation has shaken off the inseparable concomitants of that state, there must be some stage in the progress of his elevation when he takes the rank of a mere citizen, and ceases to be the special favorite of the laws, and when his rights as a citizen, or a man, are to be protected in the ordinary modes by which other men's rights are protected. There were thousands of free colored people in this country before the abolition of slavery, enjoying all the essential rights of life, liberty, and property the same as white citizens; yet no one, at that time, thought that it was any invasion of their personal *status* as freemen because they were not admitted to all the privileges enjoyed by white citizens, or because they were subjected to discriminations in the enjoyment of accommodations in inns, public conveyances, and places of amusement. Mere discriminations on account of race or color were not regarded as badges of slavery. If, since that time, the enjoyment of equal rights in all these respects has become established by constitutional enactment, it is not by force of the thirteenth amendment, (which merely abolishes slavery,) but by the force of the fourteenth and fifteenth amendments.

On the whole, we are of opinion that no countenance of authority for the passage of the law in question can be found in either the thirteenth or fourteenth amendment of the constitution; and no other ground of authority for its passage being suggested, it must necessarily be declared void, at least so far as its operation in the several states is concerned.

### Dissenting Opinion   HARLAN, J., *dissenting*.

The opinion in these cases proceeds, as it seems to me, upon grounds entirely too narrow and artificial. The substance and spirit of the recent amendments of the constitution have been sacrificed by a subtle and ingenious verbal criticism. "It is not the words of the law but the internal sense of it that makes the law. The letter of the law is the body; the sense and reason of the law is the soul." Constitutional provisions, adopted in the interest of liberty, and for the purpose of securing, through national legislation, if need be, rights inhering in a state of freedom, and belonging to American citizenship, have been so construed as to defeat the ends the people desired to accomplish, which they attempted to accomplish, and which they supposed they had accomplished by changes in their fundamental law. By this I do not mean that the determination of these cases should have been materially controlled by considerations of mere expediency or policy. I mean only, in this form, to express an earnest conviction that the court has departed from the familiar rule requiring, in the interpretation of constitutional provisions, that full effect be given to the intent with which they were adopted. . . .

The Thirteenth Amendment, it is conceded, did something more than to prohibit slavery as an *institution*, resting upon distinctions of race, and upheld by positive law. My brethren admit that it established and decreed universal *civil freedom* throughout the United States. But did the freedom thus established involve nothing more than exemption from actual slavery? Was nothing more intended than to forbid one man from owning another as property? Was it the purpose of the nation simply to destroy the institution, and then remit the race, theretofore held in bondage, to the several States for such protection, in their civil rights, necessarily growing out of freedom, as those States, in their discretion, might choose to provide? Were the States against whose protest the institution was destroyed, to be left free, so far as national interference was concerned, to make or allow discriminations against that race, as such, in the enjoyment of those fundamental rights which by universal concession, inhere in a state of freedom? Had the Thirteenth Amendment stopped with the sweeping declaration, in its first section, against the existence of slavery and involuntary servitude, except for crime, Congress would have had the power, by implication, according to the doctrines of *Prigg v. Commonwealth of Pennsylvania*, repeated in *Strauder v. West Virginia*, to protect the freedom established, and consequently, to secure the enjoyment of such civil rights as were fundamental in freedom. That it can exert its authority to that extent is made clear, and was intended to be made clear, by the express grant of power contained in the second section of the Amendment.

That there are burdens and disabilities which constitute badges of slavery and servitude, and that the power to enforce by appropriate legislation the Thirteenth Amendment may be exerted by legislation of a direct and primary character, for the eradication, not simply of the institution, but of its badges and incidents, are propositions which ought to be deemed indisputable. They lie at the foundation of the Civil Rights Act of 1866. Whether that act was authorized by the Thirteenth Amendment alone, without the support which it subsequently received from the Fourteenth Amendment, after the adoption of which it was re-enacted with some additions, my brethren do not consider it necessary to inquire. But I submit, with all respect to them, that its constitutionality is conclusively shown by their opinion. They admit, as I have said, that the Thirteenth Amendment established freedom; that there are burdens and disabilities, the necessary incidents of slavery, which constitute its substance and visible form; that Congress, by the act of 1866, passed in view of the Thirteenth Amendment, before the Fourteenth was adopted, undertook to remove certain burdens and disabilities, the necessary incidents of slavery, and to secure to all citizens of every race and color, and without regard to previous servitude, those fundamental rights which are the essence of civil freedom, namely, the same right to make and enforce contracts, to sue, be parties, give evidence, and to inherit, purchase, lease, sell, and convey property as is enjoyed by white citizens; that under the Thirteenth Amendment, Congress has to do with slavery and its incidents; and that legislation, so far as necessary or proper to eradicate all forms and incidents of slavery and involuntary servitude, may be direct and primary, operating upon the acts of individuals, whether sanctioned by State legislation or not. These propositions being conceded, it is impossible, as it seems to me, to question the constitutional validity of the Civil Rights Act of 1866. I do not contend that the Thirteenth Amendment invests Congress with authority, by legislation, to define and regulate the entire body of the civil rights which citizens enjoy, or may enjoy, in the several States. But I hold that since slavery, as the court has repeatedly declared, *Slaughter-house Cases*, 16 Wall. 36; *Strauder v. West Virginia*, 100 U.S. 303, was the moving or principal cause of the adoption of that amendment, and since that institution rested wholly upon the inferiority, as a race, of those held in bondage, their freedom necessarily involved immunity from, and protection against, all discrimination against them, because of their race, in respect of such civil rights as belong to freemen of other races. Congress, therefore, under its express power to enforce that amendment, by appropriate legislation, may enact laws to protect that people against the deprivation, because of their race, of any civil rights granted to other freemen in the same State; and such legislation may be of a direct and primary character, operating upon States, their officers and agents, and, also, upon, at least, such individuals and corporations as exercise public functions and wield power and authority under the State. . . .

For the reasons stated I feel constrained to withhold my assent to the opinion of the court.

## JONES v. ALFRED H. MAYER CO.
### *392 U.S. 409 (1968)*

MR. JUSTICE STEWART delivered the opinion of the Court.

In this case we are called upon to determine the scope and constitutionality of an Act of Congress, 42 U.S.C. § 1982, which provides that:

> "All citizens of the United States shall have the same right, in every State and Territory, as is enjoyed by white citizens thereof to inherit, purchase, lease, sell, hold, and convey real and personal property."

On September 2, 1965, the petitioners filed a complaint in the District Court for the Eastern District of Missouri, alleging that the respondents had refused to sell them a home in the Paddock Woods community of St. Louis County for the sole reason that petitioner Joseph Lee Jones is a Negro. Relying in part upon § 1982, the petitioners sought injunctive and other relief. The District Court sustained the respondents' motion to dismiss the complaint, and the Court of Appeals for the Eight Circuit affirmed, concluding that § 1982 applies only to state action and does not reach private refusals to sell. We granted certiorari to consider the questions thus presented. For the reasons that follow, we reverse the judgment of the Court of Appeals. We hold that § 1982 bars *all* racial discrimination, private as well as public, in the sale or rental of property, and that the statute, thus construed, is a valid exercise of the power of Congress to enforce the Thirteenth Amendment. . . .

We begin with the language of the statute itself. In plain and unambiguous terms, § 1982 grants to all citizens, without regard to race or color, "the same right" to purchase and lease property "as is enjoyed by white citizens." As the Court of Appeals in this case evidently recognized, that right can be impaired as effectively by "those who place property on the market" as by the State itself. For, even if the State and its agents lend no support to those who wish to exclude persons from their communities on racial grounds, the fact remains that, whenever property "is placed on the market for whites only, whites have a right denied to Negroes." So long as a Negro citizen who wants to buy or rent a home can be turned away simply because he is not white, he cannot be said to enjoy "the *same* right . . . as is enjoyed by white citizens . . . to . . . purchase [and] lease . . . real and personal property." 42 U.S.C. § 1982. (Emphasis added.)

On its face, therefore, § 1982 appears to prohibit *all* discrimination against Negroes in the sale or rental of property—discrimination by private owners as well as discrimination by public authorities. Indeed, even the respondents seem to concede that, if § 1982 "means what it says"—to use the words of the respondents' brief—then it must encompass every racially motivated refusal to sell or rent and cannot be confined to officially sanctioned segregation in housing. Stressing what they consider to be the revolutionary implications of so literal a reading of § 1982, the respondents argue that Congress cannot possibly have intended any such result. Our examination of the relevant history, however, persuades us that Congress meant exactly what it said. . . .

President Andrew Johnson vetoed the Act on March 27, and in the brief congressional debate that followed, his supporters characterized its reach in all-embracing terms. One stressed the fact that § 1 would confer "the right . . . to purchase . . . real estate . . . without any qualification and without any restriction whatever. . . ." Another predicted, as a corollary, that the Act would preclude preferential treatment for white persons in the rental of hotel rooms and in the sale of church pews. Those observations elicited no reply. On April 6 the Senate, and on April 9 the House, overrode the President's veto by the requisite majorities, and the Civil Rights Act of 1866 became law.

In light of the concerns that led Congress to adopt it and the contents of the debates that preceded its passage, it is clear that the Act was designed to do just what its terms suggest: to prohibit all racial discrimination, whether or not under color of law, with respect to the rights enumerated therein— including the right to purchase or lease property.

Nor was the scope of the 1866 Act altered when it was re-enacted in 1870, some two years after the ratification of the Fourteenth Amendment. It is quite true that some members of Congress supported the Fourteenth Amendment "in order to eliminate doubt as to the constitutional validity of the Civil Rights Act as applied to the States." *Hurd v. Hodge,* 334 U.S. 24, 32– 33. But it certainly does not follow that the adoption of the Fourteenth Amendment or the subsequent readoption of the Civil Rights Act were meant somehow to *limit* its application to state action. The legislative history furnishes not the slightest factual basis for any such speculation, and the conditions prevailing in 1870 make it highly implausible. For by that time most, if not all, of the former Confederate States, then under the control of "reconstructed" legislatures, had formally repudiated racial discrimination, and the focus of congressional concern had clearly shifted from hostile statutes to the activities of groups like the Ku Klux Klan, operating wholly outside the law. . . .

The remaining question is whether Congress has power under the Constitution to do what § 1982 purports to do: to prohibit all racial discrimination, private or public, in the sale and rental of property. Our starting point is the Thirteenth Amendment, for it was pursuant to that constitutional provision that Congress originally enacted what is now § 1982. The Amendment consists of two parts. Section 1 states:

"Neither slavery nor involuntary servitude, except as a punishment for crime whereby the party shall have been duly convicted, shall exist within the United States, or any place subject to their jurisdiction."

Section 2 provides:

"Congress shall have power to enforce this article by appropriate legislation."

As its text reveals, the Thirteenth Amendment "is not a mere prohibition of state laws establishing or upholding slavery, but an absolute declaration that slavery or involuntary servitude shall not exist in any part of the United States." *Civil Rights Cases*, 109 U.S. 3, 20. It has never been doubted, therefore, "that the power vested in Congress to enforce the article by appropriate legislation," *ibid.*, includes the power to enact laws "direct and primary, operating upon the acts of individuals, whether sanctioned by state legislation or not." *Id.*, at 23.

Thus, the fact that § 1982 operates upon the unofficial acts of private individuals, whether or not sanctioned by state law, presents no constitutional problem. If Congress has power under the Thirteenth Amendment to eradicate conditions that prevent Negroes from buying and renting property because of their race or color, then no federal statute calculated to achieve that objective can be thought to exceed the constitutional power of Congress simply because it reaches beyond state action to regulate the conduct of private individuals. The constitutional question in this case, therefore, comes to this: Does the authority of Congress to enforce the Thirteenth Amendment "by appropriate legislation" include the power to eliminate all racial barriers to the acquisition of real and personal property? We think the answer to that question is plainly yes.

"By its own unaided force and effect," the Thirteenth Amendment "abolished slavery, and established universal freedom." *Civil Rights Cases*, 109 U.S. 3, 20. Whether or not the Amendment *itself* did any more than that—a question not involved in this case—it is at least clear that the Enabling Clause of that Amendment empowered Congress to do much more. For that clause clothed "Congress with power to pass *all laws necessary and proper for abolishing all badges and incidents of slavery in the United States.*" *Ibid.* (Emphasis added.)

Those who opposed passage of the Civil Rights Act of 1866 argued in effect that the Thirteenth Amendment merely authorized Congress to dissolve the legal bond by which the Negro slave was held to his master. Yet many had earlier opposed the Thirteenth Amendment on the very ground that it would give Congress virtually unlimited power to enact laws for the protection of Negroes in every State. And the majority leaders in Congress—who were, after all, the authors of the Thirteenth Amendment—had no doubt that its Enabling Clause contemplated the sort of positive legislation that was embodied in the 1866 Civil Rights Act. Their chief spokesman, Senator Trumbull of Illinois, the Chairman of the Judiciary Committee, had brought the Thirteenth Amendment to the floor of the Senate in 1864. In defending the constitutionality of the 1866 Act, he argued that, if the narrower construction of the Enabling Clause were correct, then

> "the trumpet of freedom that we have been blowing throughout the land has given an 'uncertain sound,' and the promised freedom is a delusion. Such was not the intention of Congress, which proposed the constitutional amendment, nor is such the fair meaning of the amendment itself. ... I have no doubt that under this provision ... we may destroy all these discriminations in civil rights against the black man; and if we cannot, our constitutional amendment amounts to nothing. It was for that purpose that the second clause of that amendment was adopted, which says that Congress shall have authority, by appropriate legislation, to carry into effect the article prohibiting slavery. Who is to decide what that appropriate legislation is to be? The Congress of the United States; and it is for Congress to adopt such appropriate legislation as it may think proper, so that it be a means to accomplish the end."

Surely Senator Trumbull was right. Surely Congress has the power under the Thirteenth Amendment rationally to determine what are the badges and the incidents of slavery, and the authority to translate that determination into effective legislation. Nor can we say that the determination Congress has made is an irrational one. For this Court recognized long ago that, whatever else they may have encompassed, the badges and incidents of slavery—its "burdens and disabilities"—included restraints upon those fundamental rights which are the essence of civil freedom, namely, the same right ... to inherit, purchase, lease, sell and convey property, as is enjoyed by white citizens." *Civil Rights Cases*, 109 U.S. 3, 22. Just as the Black Codes, enacted after the Civil War to restrict the free exercise of those rights, were substitutes for the slave system, so the exclusion of Negroes from white communities became a substitute for the Black Codes. And when racial discrimination herds men into ghettos and makes their ability to buy property turn on the color of their skin, then it too is a relic of slavery.

Negro citizens, North and South, who saw in the Thirteenth Amendment a promise of freedom—freedom to "go and come at pleasure" and to "buy and sell when they please"—would be left with "a mere paper guarantee" if Congress were powerless to assure that a dollar in the hands of a Negro will purchase the same thing as a dollar in the hands of a white man. At the very least, the freedom that Congress is empowered to secure under the Thirteenth Amendment includes the freedom to buy whatever a white man can buy, the right to live wherever a white man can live. If Congress cannot say that being a free man means at least this much, then the Thirteenth Amendment made a promise the Nation cannot keep.

Representative Wilson of Iowa was the floor manager in the House for the Civil Rights Act of 1866. In urging that Congress had ample authority to pass the pending bill, he recalled the celebrated words of Chief Justice Marshall in *McCulloch v. State of Maryland*, 4 Wheat. 316, 421:

> "Let the end be legitimate, let it be within the scope of the constitution, and all means which are appropriate, which are plainly adapted to that end, which are not prohibited, but consist with the letter and spirit of the constitution, are constitutional."

"The end is legitimate," the Congressman said, "because it is defined by the Constitution itself. The end is the maintenance of freedom . . . A man who enjoys the civil rights mentioned in this bill cannot be reduced to slavery. . . . This settles the appropriateness of this measure, and that settles its constitutionality."

We agree. The judgment is reversed.

Reversed.

## DISCUSSION QUESTIONS

1. The Supreme Court decided in 1883 that Congress did not have the power to force private businesses to serve people equally regardless of race. The Court changed its mind in the 1960s. How might the history of the United States have been different if the Court had agreed with Justice Harlan in 1883 and allowed Congress to enforce laws that force private businesses to serve people equally regardless of race?

2. The Court was almost powerless to bring about racial integration in the voting booths of the South without help from Congress and the president. The same was true in the area of public accommodation. Compare Congress's effort to bring about racial integration in public schools with its efforts to bring about racial integration in the voting booth.

3. In 1974 the Supreme Court decided, in the *Milliken* decision, that as a general rule federal district judges did not have the power to order public school integration across school district boundaries. Do you think the Court would have allowed Congress to pass a law requiring federal judges to do just that? Why or why not?

# CHAPTER
# six
* * * * * * * * *

# Sex Discrimination

S cholars have argued that the Equal Protection Clause should be interpreted to mean, at a minimum, that, unless it has a very good reason for
doing so, a government should not make distinctions between groups of
people based on characteristics that people are born with and cannot do
anything about. According to this argument, it is fundamentally different to
discriminate against people who are poor (and might become rich) than to
discriminate against people because of their race or sex. The Fourteenth
Amendment certainly speaks in expansive terms. It says that "no State
shall . . . deny to any person within its jurisdiction the equal protection of the
laws." Although the Fifteenth Amendment protects the right to vote from
being denied "on account of race, color, or previous condition of servitude,"
the Fourteenth Amendment contains no such restriction. Even so, for a long
time the Court assumed that the Fourteenth Amendment only outlawed
racial discrimination and did not refer to other forms of discrimination such
as sex discrimination. The Supreme Court has not yet decided whether or
how the Equal Protection Clause applies to sexual orientation.

## SEX DISCRIMINATION AND THE ROLE OF WOMEN

It was not unreasonable for the Supreme Court to conclude that the Equal
Protection Clause did not apply to women during the second half of the
nineteenth century. When the Fourteenth Amendment was passed in 1868,
women did not have the right to vote, and in many jurisdictions under many
circumstances they could not own property or sign contracts. At the time,

people argued that the reason for the discrimination was not that women were inherently inferior, but rather that they were special. Because of their special role in society as wives and mothers, women required special treatment at the hands of government and the law.

In 1920 the Nineteenth Amendment was ratified, giving women the right to vote throughout the country in all elections. It is interesting, and significant, that the authors of the Nineteenth Amendment did not choose to place a statement in the amendment that also would guarantee women the "equal protection of the laws."

In the 1923 decision of *Adkins v. Children's Hospital*, Justice Sutherland, writing for a five-justice majority, overturned a District of Columbia law that required employers to pay women at least a minimum wage. Employers could pay men any wage, no matter how low, because there was no minimum wage for men. Justice Sutherland argued that the Nineteenth Amendment should by implication also give women equal rights to work and contract without unreasonable government interference. This decision meant women would have the same right to work for extremely low wages that men had. Justice Sutherland said:

> [W]hile the physical differences must be recognized in appropriate cases, and legislation fixing hours or conditions of work may properly take them into account, we cannot accept the doctrine that women of mature age, sui juris, require or may be subjected to restrictions upon their liberty of contract which could not lawfully be imposed in the case of men under similar circumstances.

Felix Frankfurter, who would later be appointed to the Supreme Court, argued unsuccessfully for the constitutionality of the District of Columbia's minimum wage provisions for women.

Eventually the Supreme Court seemed to abandon the idea that the Nineteenth Amendment, by implication, guaranteed women the equal protection of the law. The 1948 case of *Goesaert v. Cleary* involved a Michigan law that made it illegal for women to obtain a bartender's license unless they were "the wife or daughter of the male owner." Justice Frankfurter, who wrote the opinion for the six-member majority, viewed this case primarily as a challenge to a piece of economic regulation, not as an equal protection case. He found it to be "beyond question" that Michigan could prevent all women from working behind a bar. Therefore, the only remaining question was whether the exception for the wives and daughters of bar owners was reasonable. He concluded that it was. Justice Frankfurter stated that Michigan "evidently believes that the oversight assured through ownership of a bar by a barmaid's husband or father minimizes hazards that may confront a barmaid without such protecting oversight." Justices Douglas, Murphy, and Rutledge dissented. In his dissenting opinion, Justice Rutledge argued that the Equal Protection Clause of the Fourteenth Amendment requires "law-makers to refrain from invidious distinctions of the sort drawn by the statute challenged in this case."

## THE TURNING POINT FOR SEX DISCRIMINATION

The 1971 decision in *Reed v. Reed* marked a turning point for the Court. For the first time since the *Adkins* decision was handed down in 1923, the Supreme Court overturned a law because it denied equal protection to a woman. The case involved an Idaho law which stated that, in selecting the administrator of an estate, males should be preferred over females. When Richard Reed died, his adoptive parents, who had separated before his death, fought over who should be the administrator of their dead son's estate.

Chief Justice Burger, writing for a unanimous Court, ruled that this Idaho law favoring men over women violated the Equal Protection Clause. At the same time, he refused to say that "sex" was a "suspect classification" or that sex discrimination required any kind of special scrutiny. He argued that in this case the law simply could not meet the most basic rationality test. There was no rational reason for preferring men over women; this was simply an "arbitrary legislative choice forbidden by the Equal Protection Clause of the Fourteenth Amendment."

## THE EQUAL RIGHTS AMENDMENT

During the 1970s the states considered the Equal Rights Amendment. Passed by Congress in 1972 and sent to the states for ratification, this amendment would have read:

Section 1.  Equality of rights under the Law shall not be denied or abridged by the United States or by any state on account of sex.

Section 2.  The Congress shall have the power to enforce, by appropriate legislation, the provisions of this article.

Section 3.  The amendment shall take effect two years after the date of ratification.

The Senate report stated that the senators who voted for this amendment believed the amendment would protect both men and women from sex discrimination and that only differences mandated by the need to protect personal privacy and to recognize peculiar physical characteristics would be allowed.

The amendment was submitted to the states in early 1972, and about half the states needed for ratification approved it within a few months. It soon became clear, however, that getting the rest of the states needed would not be easy. Opponents of the ERA argued, among other things, that if the amendment became part of the Constitution families would suffer, women and men would have to share public bathrooms, and women would be subject to the draft. In 1978 Congress extended the period for ratification to 1982. On June 30, 1982, the time expired. Thirty-five states had ratified the Equal Rights Amendment, but three more were needed to make it a part of the constitution. The amendment did not become part of the Constitution.

## RECOGNIZING SEX DISCRIMINATION

In a series of decisions following *Reed*, the Court began to recognize that sex discrimination by government deserves some kind of special scrutiny. The 1973 case of *Frontiero v. Richardson* involved a rule in the U.S. military. Servicemen with wives were paid a special dependent's allowance, while servicewomen with husbands had to prove their husbands were actually dependent on them for support before receiving the allowance. Sharron Frontiero, a woman air force officer, argued that this rule deprived her of the equal protection of the law.

Justice Brennan, writing for the majority, agreed with her, arguing that sex should be considered a "suspect classification," given the history and nature of discrimination against women. While a majority of the justices agreed that the rule should be struck down (only Justice Rehnquist dissented), these justices did not all agree with Justice Brennan that sex should be considered a suspect classification.

Chief Justice Burger and Justices Stewart, Powell, and Blackmun believed that the issue of "suspect classifications" did not have to be considered to reach a decision in this case. The only justification the military gave for the rule was "administrative convenience," and this was simply not a good enough reason for discrimination, regardless of whether sex is regarded as a suspect classification. In his concurring opinion, Justice Powell argued that it was not "appropriate" for the Court to declare sex a suspect classification while the Equal Rights Amendment was being debated in state legislatures around the country.

In 1975 the Court struck down two provisions that discriminated on the basis of sex. *Weinberger v. Wisenfeld* involved Social Security rules that discriminated against widowers. Under these rules, widows could receive benefits based on their spouse's work record, but widowers could not. Stephen Wisenfeld, whose wife died in childbirth, sued Caspar Weinberger, the Secretary of Health, Education, and Welfare, to have the rule declared unconstitutional. Justice Brennan, writing for the unanimous Court, said that the distinction between widows and widowers was based on "archaic and overbroad" generalizations that should no longer apply. In the future, widows and widowers would be treated equally in terms of social security benefits.

Also in 1975, in *Stanton v. Stanton*, the Court reviewed a Utah law that required parents to support their daughters until the age of 18 and their sons until the age of 21. Justice Blackmun, writing for the eight-justice majority, ruled that this law violated the Equal Protection Clause (only Justice Rehnquist dissented).

## CREATING HEIGHTENED SCRUTINY

The Supreme Court seemed to be waiting to see whether the Equal Rights Amendment would be ratified. By 1976 it seemed unlikely that it would be. In that year, with the case of *Craig v. Boren*, the Court reviewed an Oklahoma law prohibiting the sale of "non-intoxicating" (3.2 percent alcohol) beer to males under the age of 21 and females under the age of 18. Curtis Craig, a male between the ages of 18 and 21, brought suit to have the law declared unconstitutional.

Justice Brennan began his opinion for the majority by stating that laws discriminating on the basis of sex must serve "important governmental objectives" and must be "substantially related to" the achievement of those objectives. Justice Brennan was using a new standard of scrutiny for cases involving sex discrimination. The stated reason for the discrimination in this case was to promote traffic safety. Statistics suggested that males between the ages of 18 and 21 were more likely to drive while intoxicated than females. In Justice Brennan's opinion, the evidence behind the sex discrimination in this case was not significant and the governmental objective was not strong enough to justify the discrimination.

Justices Powell, Stevens, Stewart, and Blackmun each wrote his own concurring opinion. Justices Powell and Stewart objected to the creation of a new standard of scrutiny for sex discrimination cases but found this Oklahoma law to be "irrational" under the most basic standard—the rationality test. Justices Stevens and Blackmun agreed with the basic premise of Justice

Brennan's opinion that classifications based on sex are "suspect," so government must have an important reason for making them, and they should be subject to closer scrutiny. For the first time, five justices (Brennan, Stevens, Blackmun, Marshall, and White) agreed to use some kind of heightened scrutiny for sex discrimination.

Justice Rehnquist and Chief Justice Burger dissented. In his dissenting opinion, Justice Rehnquist objected to the creation of an intermediate kind of scrutiny, somewhere between the strict scrutiny applied to race discrimination and the rationality test applied in other cases. He did not believe this new kind of scrutiny was justified. He also objected to using this new level of scrutiny to aid males, rather than females.

While race discrimination must serve a "compelling" goal, sex discrimination need only serve an "important governmental objective." Different standards are used for evaluating different types of discrimination. Although the standard used to evaluate sex discrimination is not as strict as the standard used for race discrimination, it is clearly intended to pose a higher hurdle than the simple rationality test used to evaluate other types of discrimination. We can begin to understand the different standards by looking at the cases that follow.

In the 1979 case of *Califano v. Westcott* the Court considered a section of the federal law dealing with aid to families with dependent children. This section stated that children were entitled to money if their father was unemployed but not if their mother was unemployed. Justice Brennan, who wrote the majority opinion in the five-to-four decision, argued that this rule was simply part of the "baggage of sexual stereotypes" and could not withstand the new scrutiny required in cases of sex discrimination. The rule was declared to be unconstitutional.

The 1980 case of *Wengler v. Druggists Mutual Ins. Co.* involved a Missouri worker's compensation law. The law provided automatic death benefits to a widow but required a widower to prove that he was either mentally or physically incapacitated in a way that prevented him from earning money before he could collect death benefits. When Ruth Wengler died, her husband Paul J. Wengler was denied death benefits because he could not prove he was incapable of earning a living. Justice White, who wrote the majority opinion, ruled that this provision violated the equal protection rights of working women because under the worker's compensation system their work did not earn the same benefits as work done by men. Justice White could find no "important governmental objective" to justify this different treatment. The Missouri law was overturned, and Paul J. Wengler received death benefits. Only Justice Rehnquist dissented from this conclusion.

In the 1983 case of *Arizona v. Norris,* the Court faced a state law that provided female state employees with lower monthly retirement benefits than male state employees with the same work and wage history. The Court issued a *per curiam* opinion finding that this law obviously violated the principle of equal protection.

## SEX DISCRIMINATION AND JURY DUTY

The Supreme Court has handed down three opinions about sex discrimination and jury duty over 33 years. These decisions are interesting because jury duty is considered to be a more fundamental right than the right to drink nonintoxicating beer or the right to obtain welfare. Jury duty, along with the right to vote and hold public office, is part of political equality.

In the 1961 case of *Hoyt v. State of Florida* (see p. 117), a woman, Gwendolyn Hoyt, had been convicted of murdering her husband. Florida law at the time stated that women did not have to serve on juries unless they volunteered to do so, and few did. Gwendolyn Hoyt had an all-male jury. Justice Harlan, writing for a unanimous Court, ruled that the fact that there were no women on the jury at her trial did not violate Hoyt's right to equal protection. He accepted the idea that women had "special responsibilities" that justified Florida's special procedure. Besides, women were not "positively excluded" from jury duty, they were just recruited differently from men (who were forced to serve and faced jail terms if they failed to do so). Gwendolyn Hoyt's conviction was upheld.

In the 1975 case of *Taylor v. Louisiana,* Billy Taylor, a man, was convicted by a jury of men of aggravated kidnapping. Under Louisiana law, women could serve on juries only if they filed a written declaration that they wished to serve on juries. While women made up 53 percent of the adult population of the state, very few filed the declaration. In his opinion for the majority, Justice White ruled that this method of jury selection violated Billy Taylor's right to have a jury that represented a cross section of the community. Justice White ruled that women could no longer be treated differently from men when it came to jury recruitment. Justice Rehnquist was the only dissenter. *Hoyt v. State of Florida* was overturned, along with Billy Taylor's conviction.

Finally, in April 1994, the Court again considered jury selection in *J.E.B. v. Alabama* (see p. 120). The case involved a paternity suit brought by the state of Alabama on behalf of Teresia Bible against James E. Bowman. In picking the jury, the state used its 10 peremptory challenges (challenges for which it does not have to give a reason) to strike 9 men from the available jury panel. James Bowman's attorney used his peremptory challenges to strike

10 women. The result was an all-female jury, which found that James Bowman was the father of Teresia Bible's son.

Justice Blackmun, in the majority opinion, ruled that attorneys may not use sex as the basis for making peremptory challenges any more than they may use race. He said that the guarantee of equal protection prohibits lawyers from excluding people "for no reason other than the fact that the person happens to be a woman or happens to be a man." Judges must overrule any challenges they believe to be motivated simply by a desire to remove as many males or females from the jury panel as possible. A new trial would have to be held with a new jury.

Justice Scalia dissented, joined by Chief Justice Rehnquist and Justice Thomas. Justice Scalia argued that this ruling would simply make trials longer and more expensive.

## SEX DISCRIMINATION THAT IS ACCEPTABLE

In 1981 the Court handed down two decisions that found sex discrimination to be acceptable. In *Michael M. v. Sonoma County*, a 17-year-old boy had been convicted of statutory rape. California law made it a crime for a male to have sexual intercourse with a female if the female was under the age of 18, regardless of whether or not she consented. Under this law, females involved in this illegal sexual activity were not subject to punishment. Justice Rehnquist wrote the opinion for the five-justice majority. He argued that this was not a case of sex discrimination because the state has an interest in protecting young women from becoming pregnant and causing a drain on the resources of society before they are capable of supporting a child.

Justices Brennan, White, Marshall, and Stevens dissented. Justice Brennan, in his dissenting opinion, was not convinced by this argument. He suggested that if the state's goal was to prevent teenage pregnancies it would make more sense to punish both the girl and the boy, and, in fact, punishing the girl would probably be more effective in bringing an end to teenage pregnancies and sexual intercourse by teenagers. He pointed out that 37 states already treated both sexes equally in their statutory rape laws. He argued that the real reason for the sex difference in this law was that the law was based on an outmoded sexual stereotype that young women are not capable of deciding for themselves when to have sexual intercourse.

The other 1981 decision involving acceptable sex discrimination was *Rostker v. Goldberg*. This case addressed the fact that the federal government makes males register for the draft, but not females. Justice Rehnquist, who wrote the opinion for the six-member majority, ruled that this requirement did not violate the Equal Protection Clause because the purpose of the draft is to raise an army to fight. Since at the time women were not allowed to fight in combat, he argued that it did not make sense to subject them to the draft.

Justices Brennan, White, and Marshall dissented. In his dissenting opinion, Justice White argued that women could fill many noncombat roles, and, because a modern army had more noncombat roles than combat roles, it did not make sense to exempt women from the draft. Justice Marshall pointed out in his dissenting opinion that since the decision in *Craig* the Court was required to apply heightened scrutiny in sex discrimination cases. He did not think the government's justification in this case was "substantially related" to an "important government objective."

## AFFIRMATIVE ACTION FOR WOMEN

When it comes to affirmative action plans based on race, the Court seems to require that government have a compelling reason to discriminate on the basis of race. While correcting past intentional discrimination qualifies as a compelling reason, correcting a mere social imbalance may not. Because the Court has decided that sex discrimination requires an "important" but not a "compelling" reason, it is easier to justify affirmative action on the basis of sex. Three decisions bear on this issue.

The 1977 decision of *Califano v. Webster* was a per curiam decision. The Court upheld a Social Security formula for computing old-age benefits that provided more favorable benefits for women. Women were allowed to exclude from the calculation three more low-wage years than men. This meant that they received higher retirement benefits compared with men. The Court upheld the Social Security procedure and ruled that reducing the disparity in economic conditions between men and women caused by a long history of sex discrimination in society was an "important government objective." Although sex discrimination based on archaic stereotypes was illegal, the Court stated that a desire to "redress" society's "longstanding disparate treatment of women" was an important enough reason to justify sex discrimination.

The 1982 case of *Mississippi Women's University v. Hogan* involved Joe Hogan, who tried to attend Mississippi Women's University to study nursing and was turned away because he was a man. Mississippi Women's University was founded in 1884 as the Mississippi Industrial Institute and College for the Education of White Girls. At the time Joe Hogan tried to enroll, the university had an extensive nursing program. The state of Mississippi argued that it was acceptable to limit attendance in the nursing program to women as part of an affirmative action program for women.

Justice O'Connor, the swing vote in this case, wrote the opinion for the five-justice majority. She rejected Mississippi's affirmative action argument because, at the time, 98 percent of all nurses were women. Justice O'Connor ruled that a state may not have an affirmative action program that benefits the group that already occupies the vast majority of positions in a job category. Mississippi's plan, she ruled, was intentional sex discrimination, and government needs an "exceedingly persuasive justification" for such discrimination. Helping to perpetuate the idea that women, not men, should be nurses was not persuasive enough for her or for the other justices in the majority.

Four justices dissented. Justice Powell, in his dissenting opinion, argued that this decision posed a threat to an element of diversity that has enriched both American education and American life. He pointed to the special benefits offered to women by single-sex colleges and noted that many women who could obtain admission to any college choose to attend single-sex women's colleges. In his opinion, it was wrong to deprive women of that option when it came to attending state colleges. He believed sex discrimination designed to "expand women's choices" should be allowed.

In 1987 the Court encountered another affirmative action plan for women and ruled, six to three, in its favor. The case of *Johnson v. Santa Clara County* involved sex discrimination by a county. When the job of road dispatcher came open, the county found that none of the 238 people holding jobs in the skilled-craft category were women. A panel conducted interviews and gave each applicant a score based on that interview. Seven applicants scored above 70. Paul Johnson, a white man, had the highest score, with 75. Diane Joyce, a white woman, scored 73. In order to correct the "gross underrepresentation" of women in a "traditionally segregated job category," the county gave the job to Diane Joyce. Paul Johnson sued for sex discrimination under Title VII of the 1964 Civil Rights Act. Justice Brennan wrote the opinion for the five-justice majority. He emphasized that Santa Clara's affirmative action plan was not a strict quota plan; the plan considered factors such as the sex of the applicant to be a plus if the job was one which few women held. He found this type of affirmative action plan to be acceptable.

Chief Justice Rehnquist and Justices White and Scalia dissented. These three justices objected to the use of affirmative action plans to overcome something other than intentional past discrimination by a particular governmental unit or institution.

Justice O'Connor's concurring opinion in this case is important, because she considered whether the Equal Protection Clause had been violated. Apparently, Paul Johnson had only sued under Title VII of the 1964 Civil Rights Act and had not raised the Equal Protection Clause issue. For that reason, Justice Brennan in interpreting the case focused on Title VII, and he specifically said that he did not "regard as identical the constraints of Title VII and the Federal Constitution on voluntarily adopted affirmative action plans." In other words, he left open the possibility that this plan might not be acceptable under the Equal Protection Clause.

Justice O'Connor did ask whether this kind of plan violated the Equal Protection Clause, and she found that it did not. Justice O'Connor discussed past decisions involving affirmative action and race and determined that a significant "statistical imbalance" could be used to demonstrate past discrimination by an employer. She believed the Court had not authorized affirmative action plans simply to overcome "societal discrimination," and that some proof of past discrimination by an employer was needed. In her opinion, however, a current lack of people of a particular type in a particular job category could be used to prove past discrimination.

She determined that an affirmative action plan must be remedial. Simply trying to have the percentage of women or minorities in a job category reflect the percentage of women or minorities in the labor pool is not acceptable because such a goal makes the "completely unrealistic" assumption that people of every sex and race "will gravitate with mathematical exactitude" to every job and every employer. On the other hand, if the goal takes into account the number of women and minorities who are actually "qualified for the relevant position," that could satisfy the requirement that affirmative action be "remedial" in nature. In this case, given that there were no women in the relevant job category and sex was simply "a plus factor" in the decision, Justice O'Connor believed the Equal Protection Clause had not been violated.

These three decisions suggest that real affirmative action plans designed to overcome past discrimination or gross underrepresentation of women in "traditionally segregated job categories" are acceptable because these are important enough reasons to justify sex discrimination. On the other hand, discrimination that simply perpetuates "archaic stereotypes" is not acceptable. The area of affirmative action is still unsettled, however, and four of the six justices who voted in favor of the affirmative action plan in *Johnson* are no longer on the Court. It remains to be seen how future Courts will interpret affirmative action plans.

## CONCLUSION

Members of the Supreme Court have had difficulty developing the idea that for sex discrimination some kind of intermediate, or heightened, scrutiny is called for, something between the strict scrutiny applied to race discrimination and the rationality test applied in most other discrimination cases. The Court has concluded that some kind of intermediate scrutiny is necessary. Although government does not need a *compelling* reason to justify sex discrimination, it must have an important goal, and the discrimination must appear to be closely related to the achievement of that goal.

As a result of heightened scrutiny, sex discrimination based on archaic stereotypes about the proper role of women has been declared unconstitutional in some decisions. Also, governments may discriminate in favor of women under affirmative action plans more easily than would be the case if race were involved, because race discrimination is subject to strict scrutiny, whereas sex discrimination is only subject to heightened scrutiny.

## CASE DECISIONS

In the 1961 decision of *Hoyt v. State of Florida*, the Court upheld Florida's method of selecting people for jury service, even though the Florida system discriminated against women. Justice Harlan wrote the opinion for the unanimous Court, which is included here. Chief Justice Warren's short concurring opinion is also included.

In the 1994 decision of *J.E.B. v. Alabama*, the Court ruled, six to three, that government attorneys may not use their right to strike jurors from a jury panel to discriminate against men or women because of their sex. Justice Blackmun's opinion for the majority is included here. Justices O'Connor and Kennedy wrote concurring opinions, and Chief Justice Rehnquist and Justice Scalia wrote dissenting opinions. These opinions are not included here.

Following are excerpts from the case decisions.

❀ ❀ ❀ ❀ ❀ ❀ ❀ ❀

## HOYT v. STATE OF FLORIDA
### 368 U.S. 57 (1961)

MR. JUSTICE HARLAN delivered the opinion of the Court.

Appellant, a woman, has been convicted in Hillsborough County, Florida, of second degree murder of her husband. On this appeal under 28 U.S.C. § 1257 (2), 28 U.S.C.A. § 1257(2), from the Florida Supreme Court's affirmance of the judgment of conviction, 119 So.2d 691, we noted probable jurisdiction, 364 U.S. 930, to consider appellant's claim that her trial before an all-male jury violated her rights assured by the Fourteenth Amendment. The claim is that such jury was the product of a state jury statute which works an unconstitutional exclusion of women from jury service.

The jury law primarily in question is Fla.Stat., 1959, § 40.01(1), F.S.A. This Act, which requires that grand and petit jurors be taken from "male and female" citizens of the State possessed of certain qualifications, contains the following proviso:

> "provided, however, that the name of no female person shall be taken for jury service unless said person has registered with the clerk of the circuit court her desire to be placed on the jury list."

Showing that since the enactment of the statute only a minimal number of women have so registered, appellant challenges the constitutionality of the statute both on its face and as applied in this case. For reasons now to follow we decide that both contentions must be rejected.

At the core of appellant's argument is the claim that the nature of the crime of which she was convicted peculiarly demanded the inclusion of persons of her own sex on the jury. She was charged with killing her husband by assaulting him with a baseball bat. . . .

Of course, these premises misconceive the scope of the right to an impartially selected jury assured by the Fourteenth Amendment. That right does not entitle one accused of crime to a jury tailored to the circumstances of the particular case, whether relating to the sex or other condition of the defendant, or to the nature of the charges to be tried. It requires only that the jury be indiscriminately drawn from among those eligible in the community for jury service, untrammelled by any arbitrary and systematic exclusions. . . .

In the selection of jurors Florida has differentiated between men and women in two respects. It has given women an absolute exemption from jury duty based solely on their sex, no similar exemption obtaining as to men. And it has provided for its effectuation in a manner less onerous than that governing exemptions exercisable by men: women are not to be put on the jury list unless they have voluntarily registered for such service; men, on the other hand, even if entitled to an exemption, are to be included on the list unless they have filed a written claim of exemption as provided by law. Fla.Stat., 1959, § 40.10, F.S.A.

In neither respect can we conclude that Florida's statute is not "based on some reasonable classification," and that it is thus infected with unconstitutionality. Despite the enlightened emancipation of women from the restrictions and protections of bygone years, and their entry into many parts of community life formerly considered to be reserved to men, woman is still regarded as the center of home and family life. We cannot say that it is constitutionally impermissible for a State, acting in pursuit of the general welfare, to conclude that a woman should be relieved from the civic duty of jury service unless she herself determines that such service is consistent with her own special responsibilities.

Florida is not alone in so concluding. Women are now eligible for jury service in all but three States of the Union. Of the forty-seven States where women are eligible, seventeen besides Florida, as well as the District of Columbia, have accorded women an absolute exemption based solely on their sex, exercisable in one form or another. In two of these States, as in Florida, the exemption is automatic, unless a woman volunteers for such service. It is true, of course, that Florida could have limited the exemption, as some other States have done, only to women who have family responsibilities. But we cannot regard it as irrational for a state legislature to consider preferable a broad exemption, whether born of the State's historic public policy or of a determination that it would not be administratively feasible to decide in each individual instance whether the family responsibilities of a prospective female juror were serious enough to warrant an exemption. . . .

Appellant argues that whatever may have been the design of this Florida enactment, the statute in practical operation results in an exclusion of women from jury service, because women, like men, can be expected to be available for jury service only under compulsion. In this connection she points out that by 1957, when this trial took place, only some 220 women out of approximately 46,000 registered female voters in Hillsborough County—constituting about 40 per cent of the total voting population of that county—had volunteered for jury duty since the limitation of jury service to males, see *Hall v. Florida*, 136 Fla. 644, 662–665, 187 So. 392, 400–401, was removed by § 40.01(1) in 1949. Fla.Laws 1949, c. 25126.

This argument, however, is surely beside the point. Given the reasonableness of the classification involved in § 40.01(1), the relative paucity of women jurors does not carry the constitutional consequence appellant would have it bear. "Circumstances or chance may well dictate that no persons in a certain case will serve on a particular jury or during some particular period." *Hernandez v. Texas, supra*, 347 U.S. at 482, 74 S. Ct. at 672.

We cannot hold this statute as written offensive to the Fourteenth Amendment.

**Concurring Opinion**  THE CHIEF JUSTICE, MR. JUSTICE BLACK and MR. JUSTICE DOUGLAS, concurring.

We cannot say from this record that Florida is not making a good faith effort to have women perform jury duty without discrimination on the ground of sex. . . .

## J.E.B. v. ALABAMA
### 114 S. Ct. 1419 (1994)

JUSTICE BLACKMUN delivered the opinion of the Court.

In *Batson v. Kentucky*, 476 U.S. 79 (1986), this Court held that the Equal Protection Clause of the Fourteenth Amendment governs the exercise of peremptory challenges by a prosecutor in a criminal trial. The Court explained that although a defendant has "no right to a 'petit jury composed in whole or in part of persons of his own race' " *id.*, at 85, quoting *Strauder v. West Virginia*, 100 U.S. 303, 305 (1880), the "defendant does have the right to be tried by a jury whose members are selected pursuant to nondiscriminatory criteria." *Id.*, 476 U.S., at 85–86. Since *Batson*, we have reaffirmed repeatedly our commitment to jury selection procedures that are fair and nondiscriminatory. We have recognized that whether the trial is criminal or civil, potential jurors, as well as litigants, have an equal protection right to jury selection procedures that are free from state-sponsored group stereotypes rooted in, and reflective of, historical prejudice. . . .

Although premised on equal protection principles that apply equally to gender discrimination, all our recent cases defining the scope of *Batson* involved alleged racial discrimination in the exercise of peremptory challenges. Today we are faced with the question whether the Equal Protection Clause forbids intentional discrimination on the basis of gender, just as it prohibits discrimination on the basis of race. We hold that gender, like race, is an unconstitutional proxy for juror competence and impartiality.

On behalf of relator T.B., the mother of a minor child, respondent State of Alabama filed a complaint for paternity and child support against petitioner J.E.B. in the District Court of Jackson County, Alabama. On October 21, 1991, the matter was called for trial and jury selection began. The trial court assembled a panel of 36 potential jurors, 12 males and 24 females. After the court excused three jurors for cause, only 10 of the remaining 33 jurors were male. The State then used 9 of its 10 peremptory strikes to remove male jurors; petitioner used all but one of his strikes to remove female jurors. As a result, all the selected jurors were female.

Before the jury was empaneled, petitioner objected to the State's peremptory challenges on the ground that they were exercised against male jurors solely on the basis of gender, in violation of the Equal Protection Clause of the Fourteenth Amendment. Petitioner argued that the logic and reasoning of *Batson v. Kentucky*, which prohibits peremptory strikes solely on the basis of race, similarly forbids intentional discrimination on the basis of gender. The court rejected petitioner's claim and empaneled the all-female jury. The jury found petitioner to be the father of the child and the court entered an order directing him to pay child support. On post-judgment motion, the court reaffirmed its ruling that *Batson* does not extend to gender-based peremptory challenges. . . .

Today we reaffirm what, by now, should be axiomatic: Intentional discrimination on the basis of gender by state actors violates the Equal Protection Clause, particularly where, as here, the discrimination serves to ratify and perpetuate invidious, archaic, and overbroad stereotypes about the relative abilities of men and women. . . .

Discrimination in jury selection, whether based on race or on gender, causes harm to the litigants, the community, and the individual jurors who are wrongfully excluded from participation in the judicial process. The litigants are harmed by the risk that the prejudice which motivated the discriminatory selection of the jury will infect the entire proceedings. See *Edmonson*, 500 U.S., at 614, (discrimination in the courtroom "raises serious questions as to the fairness of the proceedings conducted there"). The community is harmed by the State's participation in the perpetuation of invidious group stereotypes and the inevitable loss of confidence in our judicial system that state-sanctioned discrimination in the courtroom engenders.

When state actors exercise peremptory challenges in reliance on gender stereotypes, they ratify and reinforce prejudicial views of the relative abilities of men and women. Because these stereotypes have wreaked injustice in so many other spheres of our country's public life, active discrimination by litigants on the basis of gender during jury selection "invites cynicism respecting the jury's neutrality and its obligation to adhere to the law." *Powers v. Ohio*, 499 U.S., at 412. The potential for cynicism is particularly acute in cases where gender-related issues are prominent, such as cases involving rape, sexual harassment, or paternity. Discriminatory use of peremptory challenges may create the impression that the judicial system has acquiesced in suppressing full participation by one gender or that the "deck has been stacked" in favor of one side. See *id.*, at 413 ("The verdict will not be accepted or understood [as fair] if the jury is chosen by unlawful means at the outset"). . . .

Equal opportunity to participate in the fair administration of justice is fundamental to our democratic system. It not only furthers the goals of the jury system. It reaffirms the promise of equality under the law—that all citizens, regardless of race, ethnicity, or gender, have the chance to take part directly in our democracy. *Powers v. Ohio*, 499 U.S., at 407 ("Indeed, with the exception of voting, for most citizens the honor and privilege of jury duty is their most significant opportunity to participate in the democratic process"). When persons are excluded from participation in our democratic processes solely because of race or gender, this promise of equality dims, and the integrity of our judicial system is jeopardized.

In view of these concerns, the Equal Protection Clause prohibits discrimination in jury selection on the basis of gender, or on the assumption that an individual will be biased in a particular case for no reason other than the fact that the person happens to be a woman or happens to be a man. As with race, the "core guarantee of equal protection, ensuring citizens that their State will not discriminate . . ., would be meaningless were we to approve the exclusion of jurors on the basis of such assumptions, which arise solely from the jurors' [gender]." *Batson*, 476 U.S., at 97–98.

The judgment of the Court of Civil Appeals of Alabama is reversed and the case is remanded to that court for further proceedings not inconsistent with this opinion.

*It is so ordered.*

## ················DISCUSSION QUESTIONS················

1. Do you think it was an abuse of power for the Supreme Court to decide that the Equal Protection Clause protects women when the United States refused to ratify the Equal Rights Amendment?

2. The Supreme Court decided in 1981 that Congress could draft men and not draft women without violating the principle of equal protection because women did not fill combat roles in the military. In 1994 women were allowed to serve on navy combat ships for the first time. Given that fact, do you think the draft now does discriminate against men because the major rationale for the sex difference no longer exists?

3. Chief Justice Rehnquist has argued that the concept of equal protection should not be used to protect men as well as women from sex discrimination. Do you think it would be acceptable to use equal protection to protect women but not men from sex discrimination? The Court has consistently said that the concept of equal protection protects white people from race discrimination as well as minorities. Why should the rule be different when it comes to protecting men?

4. It can be argued that affirmative action plans that aid women do not have to survive the same scrutiny as affirmative action plans that help minorities because sex discrimination only calls for heightened scrutiny, not strict scrutiny. Heightened scrutiny means government must have an important reason for the discrimination, whereas strict scrutiny means government must have a compelling reason. The desire to correct the effect of past discrimination might qualify as an important reason where it might not qualify as a compelling reason. However, in the *Johnson* case, Justice O'Connor seemed to approach the issue of an affirmative action plan for women in the same way she approaches affirmative action plans for minorities. Does this suggest that she is now using strict scrutiny in sex discrimination cases? If so, is this good or bad? Do you think other justices will take the same approach? Is it fair to subject affirmative action plans that help women to strict scrutiny but only subject procedures and laws which hurt women to heightened scrutiny?

5. What if the Court had continued to believe that the Nineteenth Amendment implied that women should receive the equal protection of the laws, as it did in the 1923 *Adkins* decision? How might the legal history of the twentieth century have been different?

# CHAPTER
## seven
❋❋❋❋❋❋❋❋❋

# Urban Residence and Poverty

···················· DISCUSSION ·····························

Two other categories of equal protection decisions involve people who live in urban areas and people who happen to be poor. These characteristics are different from race or sex—they can be changed. In considering discrimination cases based on urban residence or poverty, the Court has focused on the kinds of rights and privileges government was trying to deny. The Court has most often decided in favor of equal protection in those cases involving fundamental political rights, such as the right to vote, run for office, or make use of the judicial system.

### URBAN DWELLERS AND THE RIGHT TO VOTE

In the early 1900s, many states stopped reapportioning state legislative or congressional districts. Reapportionment occurs when districts are redrawn to reflect changes in population. If reapportionment is not done, some people's votes will count more than other people's. People were moving into the states from outside, and most of the new residents moved into large cities such as Chicago or Atlanta. People who lived in rural areas in many states soon realized that in time newcomers might outnumber them and take control of the state government, so the states stopped reapportioning. During the first half of the twentieth century, this failure to reapportion legislative and congressional districts resulted in greater and greater discrepancies between the relative voting power of rural and urban dwellers.

The 1946 case of *Colegrove v. Green*, handed down by the New Deal Court, illustrates the problem. In Illinois, congressional districts had not been redrawn since 1900. As a result, one rural district contained 112,000 people, whereas one urban district contained 914,000 people. The majority of justices refused to do anything about the situation. Justice Frankfurter, who wrote the opinion for the six-justice majority, argued that the imbalance between rural and urban districts was a political problem and the Supreme Court was not in a position to provide a remedy.

Justices Black, Douglas, and Murphy dissented. In his dissenting opinion, Justice Black pointed to several provisions in the Constitution that he believed gave the Court the power to correct the problem. First, the Equal Protection Clause of the Fourteenth Amendment suggests that the authors of the amendment believed that people's votes would have an equal impact. Second, the Privileges or Immunities Clause of the Fourteenth Amendment should mean that each person should have an equally powerful vote. The Privileges and Immunities Clause says that states may not abridge the privileges and immunities of citizens, including, presumably, the privilege to cast a meaningful vote. Third, Article I of the Constitution, which calls for a census every 10 years for the purpose of dividing up congressional seats, implies that new districts should be drawn to reflect the results of that census.

## ONE PERSON, ONE VOTE

The Court reconsidered the reapportionment issue in 1964, in *Wesberry v. Sanders*, after many changes in the makeup of the Court. The case involved congressional districts in Georgia. These districts had not been redrawn since 1930, and one district had three times more people in it than another district. Justice Black wrote a majority opinion forcing Georgia (and by implication many other states) to reapportion its congressional districts. He ruled that Article I, Section 2, of the Constitution, which says that congressional representatives will be chosen "by the people," means that congressional districts must be drawn, to the fullest extent possible, on the basis of the principle of "one person, one vote." Only Justices Harlan and Stewart dissented.

*Reynolds v. Sims*, another 1964 case, also involved reapportionment. In this case, state legislative districts, rather than congressional districts, were in question. In Alabama, state senators represented regions of the state, just as United States senators represent states. Alabama had not redrawn its state legislative districts since 1900. Chief Justice Warren, writing for the Court, ordered that new districts reflecting the actual population of the state rather than regional boundaries be drawn for both houses of the Alabama legislature. This meant that in states such as Alabama the practice of senators representing regions would have to come to an end. In coming to this conclusion, the chief justice said, "legislatures represent people, not trees or acres." In this and several other cases decided on the same day, the Court rejected the idea that such an unequal apportionment could be legitimate, even if called for in the state constitution. Only Justice Harlan dissented. In 1968 the Court made it clear that even county commissioner districts must be based on population, not area (*Avery v. Midland County*).

Chief Justice Warren considered these decisions to be the most important decisions handed down by the Warren Court. They certainly had the most far-reaching effect. Urban dwellers in states such as Illinois and Georgia suddenly found themselves in control of the state legislature and the state's congressional delegation. Much of the civil rights legislation passed by Congress after these decisions would probably not have been possible without the congressional redistricting that resulted from these decisions.

In the years that followed, the Court has generally been willing to allow for more population deviation when drawing state legislative districts than when drawing congressional districts. For example, in *Mahan v. Howell* the Court allowed Virginia to take local political subdivisions into account even though it resulted in a 16 percent variation in the size of the districts. In *Brown v. Thompson* the Court allowed Wyoming to have legislative districts with an 89 percent variation in population size in order to respect county boundaries. On the other hand, the Court has consistently required congressional districts to be as nearly equal in population as possible.

## EQUAL PROTECTION FOR THE POOR

The idea that poor people might have some right to equal protection begins with the concept of due process, not the concept of equal protection. In the 1956 case of *Griffin v. Illinois*, Justice Black, writing for the five-justice majority, ruled that it was a violation of due process of law to deny a poor criminal defendant the right to appeal his conviction because he could not afford to pay for a trial transcript. In the 1959 case of *Burns v. Ohio*, Chief Justice Warren, writing for the seven-justice majority, ruled that it was a denial of equal protection for the state of Ohio to require poor people who wished to appeal their conviction to the Ohio Supreme Court to pay a fee. Finally, in 1963, a unanimous Supreme Court ruled that a poor criminal defendant had a right to a court-appointed attorney in *Gideon v. Wainwright*.

## THE POOR AND ACCESS TO GOVERNMENT

In the early 1970s the Court drew the line between what kind of access to government was fundamental enough to require government to either waive a fee or provide assistance for the poor and what kind of access was not. In the 1971 opinion in *Boddie v. Connecticut*, the eight-justice majority ruled that a state could not keep poor people from obtaining a divorce simply because they could not come up with the $60 filing fee. In 1973, with two five-to-four votes, the Court ruled that government could require poor people to pay a fee to file for bankruptcy or to appeal the denial of welfare benefits (*United States v. Kras; Ortwein v. Schwab*). The conclusion was that the right to get a divorce was more fundamental than the right to file for bankruptcy or the right to appeal the denial of welfare benefits.

## POLITICAL EQUALITY AND THE POOR

The Court, in a series of decisions, has ruled that voting and running for office are such fundamental rights that a state needs a compelling reason to limit the right of poor people to engage in these activities. As a general rule, states have not been able to come up with a compelling enough reason for discriminating against poor people in these areas.

In the 1966 case of *Harper v. Virginia Board of Elections*, Justice Douglas, writing for a six-justice majority, ruled that Virginia's poll tax was unconstitutional. Even though Virginia's poll tax was only $1.50, that was too much. Justice Douglas ruled that wealth, like race, creed, and color, had no connection with the ability to cast a vote. Because the right to vote is so fundamental, any restriction of it is subject to strict scrutiny, even if the restriction is not based on race.

In 1972 and 1974, in two opinions written by Chief Justice Burger for unanimous courts, the Court outlawed the use of filing fees to run for public office (*Bullock v. Carter; Lubin v. Panish*). Poor people have just as much right to run for public office as everyone else; this is a fundamental right.

In almost every case the Court has struck down requirements that people must own property before they may vote in an election. In the first such case, *Kramer v. Union School District*, decided in 1969, Chief Justice Warren, writing for a six-member majority, ruled that property restrictions on voting violated the Equal Protection Clause of the Fourteenth Amendment. In this case people were only allowed to vote in the school board election if they owned or leased taxable property in the district or had a child attending the district's schools. The chief justice ruled that this requirement limited the fundamental right to vote on the basis of wealth and was therefore unconstitutional.

In two cases the Court ruled that bond elections could not be limited to people who "owned property" or people who "paid property taxes" (*Cipriano v. Houma; Hill v. Stone*). In the 1989 case of *Quinn v. Millsap*, Justice Blackmun, writing for a unanimous Court, ruled that a provision in the constitution of Missouri that called for a board made up only of property owners to draft a plan of reorganization for the government of the city of St. Louis was unconstitutional.

The only time the Court has allowed a property requirement for voting has been in elections for a water district board of directors (*Salyer Land Co. v. Tulare Water District*). In that case the Court accepted the argument that because only land owners pay for water only they should be able to vote for who should sit on the water district board.

## PUBLIC EDUCATION AND THE POOR

As a general rule, the right to a public education has not been considered to be as fundamental as the right to vote or run for public office. The Supreme Court has frequently said that nothing in the U.S. Constitution requires states to provide a free public education. At the same time, the Court has obviously viewed public education as special, not as the equivalent of a public swimming pool or city-owned recreational facility. In 1973 the Supreme Court seriously considered overturning the way most states finance public schools, but decided against it with a vote of five-to-four.

Mexican American parents of children in the Edgewood School District in San Antonio, Texas, sued the state of Texas in the case of *San Antonio School District v. Rodriguez* (see p. 133). They argued that the way Texas financed public education discriminated against children who resided in poor school districts. Although the state provided some funds to support education, the bulk of financing came from local property taxes. That meant children who lived in districts with high-value property received a much better education than children who lived in districts with low-value property. The Mexican American parents pointed to the Alamo Heights School District as an example. The average assessed property value in the Edgewood District was $5,960. The average assessed property value in the Alamo Heights District was $49,000. This resulted in an average per pupil expenditure (after receiving state and federal funds) of $356 in Edgewood and $594 in Alamo Heights, even though the Edgewood District taxed property at a higher property tax rate than Alamo Heights.

Justice Powell began his opinion for the majority by overruling the federal district judge who had found wealth to be a "suspect" classification and education to be a "fundamental interest." Justice Powell rejected both of these conclusions. He ruled that the Supreme Court had never found wealth alone to be a suspect classification or education to be a fundamental right. He argued that there are only two kinds of equal protection analysis: strict scrutiny, which is used when suspect classifications such as race or fundamental interests such as the right to vote are involved, and the rationality test. He rejected the idea that the Court had developed types of equal protection analysis that fell in between, what some had called "heightened" scrutiny. He then considered whether Texas could justify the way it financed public education with some kind of rational explanation.

Justice Powell pointed out that this was not exactly a case of discrimination against poor children. These children were being discriminated against because of where they lived, not because, as individuals, they were either rich or poor. In his opinion, this case was similar to cases where urban dwellers were deprived of a right to vote. Also, being in a rich or poor school district did not result in "an absolute deprivation of the desired benefit." Children in a poor district were still receiving a free public education; they were just not getting the same education provided to children in rich districts. Because of these factors, Justice Powell believed that the discrimination in this case simply had to pass the "rationality" test.

Justice Powell then asked whether Texas had a rational, nonarbitrary reason for treating these children differently. Texas's reason was that it wanted to allow for local control over public education. Justice Powell accepted this as a rational reason to finance public education in the traditional way. He also emphasized that the Supreme Court had generally not interfered with how a state chooses to spend its money.

Justices Douglas, Brennan, White, and Marshall dissented. Justice White, in his dissenting opinion, criticized the way Justice Powell and the majority applied the "rationality test" in this case. Justice White objected to the fact that the state of Texas put limits on how much property tax revenue districts could raise and did not provide enough funds from the state to provide a basic level of funding. In his opinion, Justice Powell had not correctly applied the rationality test because he had not asked Texas to prove that its "unequal treatment" of children was rationally related to the achievement of its stated goal, furthering local control of public education. He did not see why local control would necessarily be lost if some other method of financing public education were used.

In his dissent, Justice Marshall argued that the majority of justices had ignored the fact that the Court had developed a much more complex equal protection analysis over the years. He said:

> The Court apparently seeks to establish today that equal protection cases fall into one of two neat categories which dictate the appropriate standard of review—strict scrutiny or mere rationality. But this Court's decisions . . . defy such easy categorization. A principled reading of what this Court has done reveals that it has applied a spectrum of standards in reviewing discrimination allegedly violative of the Equal Protection Clause. This spectrum clearly comprehends variations in the degree of care with which the Court will scrutinize particular classifications, depending, I believe, on the constitutional and societal importance of the interest adversely affected and the recognized invidiousness of the basis upon which the particular classification is drawn.

Justice Marshall then went on to argue that discrimination based on wealth deserved heightened scrutiny and that discrimination that resulted in significant differences in public education also deserved heightened scrutiny. He did not believe Texas's reason was important enough to justify the discrimination in this case. The state of Texas could have allowed local school boards to maintain control of the education system and at the same time taken steps to minimize the effect that disparities in property tax valuation had on the system.

Nearly a decade later, in 1982, the Court faced another discrimination case involving public education. The Court again voted five to four, but this time in favor of the children who had been deprived of a public education. The case, *Plyler v. Doe* (see p. 139), involved a lawsuit brought on behalf of illegal alien children who were being denied a public education in Texas.* Justice Brennan wrote the opinion for the Court. He turned first to the exact wording of the Fourteenth Amendment, which says that no state shall deny "to any person within its jurisdiction" the equal protection of the laws. Clearly, these children were within the jurisdiction of Texas. He then pointed to the fact that "sheer incapability or lax enforcement" had "resulted in the creation of a substantial 'shadow population' of illegal migrants" that numbered in the millions. Justice Brennan believed this situation raised the "specter of a permanent caste of undocumented resident aliens, encouraged by some to remain" to provide cheap labor while the benefits of the society were not made available to them. Justice Brennan argued that, although public education is not a "right" granted by the Constitution, it is not "merely some governmental 'benefit' indistinguishable from other forms of social welfare." Following Justice Powell's decision in *Rodriguez*, Justice Brennan

---

*Editor's Note:* In November 1994, Californians voted to deny illegal immigrants access to education and most health care. Lawsuits have already been filed against this proposition, and it is possible that this issue will be taken to the Supreme Court.

applied the rationality test and found that Texas's only stated reason for denying a public education to illegal aliens—to save money—was not a good enough reason.

Justice Blackmun wrote his own concurring opinion to emphasize that he accepted the idea that there were more than two types of equal protection analysis. Where certain classifications and particular rights are concerned, he believed the Court had applied, and should apply, a stricter test than simply requiring the state to come up with some kind of rational reason for its actions.

Justice Powell also wrote a concurring opinion for the same reason. He argued that there were different categories of equal protection analysis, contradicting his own opinion in the *San Antonio School District v. Rodriguez* case. In his opinion, this case called for "heightened" scrutiny. To pass a heightened scrutiny test, Texas would have to have "substantial" interests at stake and would have to demonstrate that its discriminatory practices had a "fair and substantial relation" to these interests. He believed that Texas could not meet this test. He stated that Texas's "denial of education to these children bears no substantial relation to any substantial state interest." Instead, Justice Powell argued, this was discrimination based on the "status" of the children involved and violated the Equal Protection Clause.

Chief Justice Burger wrote a dissenting opinion, joined by Justices White, Rehnquist, and O'Connor. He argued that it is not the Court's business to "set the Nation's social policy." While he agreed "without hesitation" that it is "senseless for an enlightened society to deprive any children—including illegal aliens—of an elementary education," he thought it was an abuse of the Court's power to force society to provide a public education to illegal aliens. The Supreme Court cannot become the "omnipotent and omniscient" solver of all of society's problems.

Chief Justice Burger then turned to the analysis used by the five-justice majority in this case. In his opinion, what they had actually done was spin "out a theory custom-tailored to the facts" of the case. He went on to say:

> In the end, we are told little more than that the level of scrutiny employed to strike down the Texas law applies only when illegal alien children are deprived of a public education. If ever a court was guilty of an unabashedly result-oriented approach, this case is a prime example.

The chief justice also argued that the majority had ignored the reason these children were being denied a public education: they are in the country illegally. He then argued that the Court had misapplied the rationality test. In his opinion, it "simply is not irrational for a State to conclude that it does not have the same responsibility to provide benefits for persons whose very presence in the State and this country is illegal as it does to provide for persons lawfully" residing in the country. He believed that it was rational for a state to wish to use its limited revenue to serve the needs of lawful residents.

_ Chief Justice Burger objected to what he called the "result-oriented approach" taken by the majority. Every equal protection decision handed down in the second half of the twentieth century, however, has to some degree been result-oriented, if by that we mean that the justices have looked at the fundamental values of the society and used their interpretation of those fundamental values to make concrete decisions. In equal protection decisions, three values appear to be dominant: the value of equal participation in the political process, the value of economic opportunity, and the belief that the sins of the ancestors should not be visited on their descendants. In the *Plyler* case, two of these values were directly involved, and the third, the value of equal participation in the political process, was indirectly involved in that people without education can not meaningfully participate in the political process.

## CONCLUSION

The Supreme Court ultimately had to address the fact that basic political equality was being denied to millions of people because they happened to be poor or they happened to live in a large city. The problem became too great for the Court to ignore. To correct the problem, the Court decided that some rights, such as the right to vote, hold public office, or use the judicial system, were too important to be provided to people on an unequal basis, even when the reason for the discrimination was not based on race. At the same time, there was certainly an undercurrent of race in some of these decisions. Many of the poor or urban dwellers were also members of racial minorities. The Court ruled that basic political equality was too important, too fundamental, to be parceled out in an unequal way.

The Court has had to struggle to determine which kind of scrutiny should be applied to cases that involve discrimination based on poverty or place of residence rather than on race or sex. Although some justices have tried to argue that there are only two kinds of scrutiny, strict scrutiny and the rationality test, it is clear that the Court has used other types of analysis in discrimination cases. It is also clear that many justices have looked at the basic values involved in a particular case and decided that the fundamental values of the society demanded a particular result. While such a result-oriented approach has been criticized by scholars and the justices themselves, it is doubtful that any other approach was possible.

## CASE DECISIONS

In the 1973 decision of *San Antonio School District v. Rodriguez*, the Supreme Court refused to overturn the way Texas, and most states, financed public schools even though it discriminates against people who live in poor school districts. Justice Powell wrote the opinion for the five-justice majority, and his opinion is included here. Justice Stewart's concurring opinion is also included, as is Justice Marshall's dissenting opinion. Dissenting opinions by Justices Brennan and White are not included.

In the 1982 decision of *Plyler v. Doe*, the Court decided that states may not refuse to provide a public education to students simply because they are illegal aliens. Justice Brennan's opinion for the five-justice majority is included here. The concurring opinions of Justices Marshall, Blackmun, and Powell and Chief Justice Burger's dissenting opinion are not included.

Following are excerpts from the case decisions.

❋ ❋ ❋ ❋ ❋ ❋ ❋ ❋ ❋

## SAN ANTONIO SCHOOL DISTRICT v. RODRIGUEZ
### *411 U.S. 1 (1973)*

MR. JUSTICE POWELL delivered the opinion of the Court.

The District Court's opinion does not reflect the novelty and complexity of the constitutional questions posed by appellees' challenge to Texas' system of school financing. In concluding that strict judicial scrutiny was required, that court relied on decisions dealing with the rights of indigents to equal treatment in the criminal trial and appellate processes, and on cases disapproving wealth restrictions on the right to vote. Those cases, the District Court concluded, established wealth as a suspect classification. Finding that the local property tax system discriminated on the basis of wealth, it regarded those precedents as controlling. It then reasoned, based on decisions of this Court affirming the undeniable importance of education, that there is a fundamental right to education and that, absent some compelling state justification, the Texas system could not stand.

We are unable to agree that this case, which in significant aspects is *sui generis*, may be so neatly fitted into the conventional mosaic of constitutional analysis under the Equal Protection Clause. Indeed, for the several reasons that follow, we find neither the suspect-classification nor the fundamental-interest analysis persuasive.

The wealth discrimination discovered by the District Court in this case, and by several other courts that have recently struck down school-financing laws in other States, is quite unlike any of the forms of wealth discrimination heretofore reviewed by this Court. Rather than focusing on the unique features of the alleged discrimination, the courts in these cases have virtually assumed their findings of a suspect classification through a simplistic process of analysis: since, under the traditional systems of financing public schools, some poorer people receive less expensive educations than other more afflu-ent people, these systems discriminate on the basis of wealth. This approach largely ignores the hard threshold questions, including whether it makes a difference for purposes of consideration under the Constitution that the class of disadvantaged "poor" cannot be identified or defined in customary equal protection terms, and whether the relative—rather than absolute—nature of the asserted deprivation is of significant consequence. Before a State's laws and the justifications for the classifications they create are subjected to strict judicial scrutiny, we think these threshold considerations must be analyzed more closely than they were in the court below.

The case comes to us with no definitive description of the classifying facts or delineation of the disfavored class. Examination of the District Court's opinion and of appellees' complaint, briefs, and contentions at oral argument suggests, however, at least three ways in which the discrimination claimed here might be described. The Texas system of school financing might be regarded as discriminating (1) against "poor" persons whose incomes fall below some identifiable level of poverty or who might be characterized as functionally "indigent," or (2) against those who are relatively poorer than others, or (3) against all those who, irrespective of their personal incomes, happen to reside in relatively poorer school districts. Our task must be to ascertain whether, in fact, the Texas system has been shown to discriminate on any of these possible bases and, if so, whether the resulting classification may be regarded as suspect. . . .

Only appellees' first possible basis for describing the class disadvantaged by the Texas school-financing system—discrimination against a class of defin-ably "poor" persons—might arguably meet the criteria established in these prior cases. Even a cursory examination, however, demonstrates that neither of the two distinguishing characteristics of wealth classifications can be found here. First, in support of their charge that the system discriminates against the "poor," appellees have made no effort to demonstrate that it operates to the peculiar disadvantage of any class fairly definable as indigent, or as composed of persons whose incomes are beneath any designated poverty level. Indeed, there is reason to believe that the poorest families are not necessarily clustered in the poorest property districts. A recent and exhaustive study of school districts in Connecticut concluded that "[i]t is clearly incorrect . . . to contend that the 'poor' live in 'poor' districts. . . . Thus, the major factual assumption of *Serrano*—that the educational financing system discriminates against the 'poor'—is simply false in Connecticut." Defining "poor" families as those below the Bureau of the Census "poverty level," the Connecticut study found, not surprisingly, that the poor were clustered around commercial and industrial areas—those same areas that provide the most attractive sources of property tax income for school districts. Whether a similar pattern would be discovered in Texas is not known, but there is no basis on the record in this case for assuming that the poorest people—defined by reference to any level of absolute impecunity—are concentrated in the poorest districts.

Second, neither appellees nor the District Court addressed the fact that, unlike each of the foregoing cases, lack of personal resources has not occasioned an absolute deprivation of the desired benefit. The argument here is not that the children in districts having relatively low assessable property values are receiving no public education; rather, it is that they are receiving a poorer quality education than that available to children in districts having more assessable wealth. Apart from the unsettled and disputed question whether the quality of education may be determined by the amount of money expended for it, a sufficient answer to appellees' argument is that, at least where wealth is involved, the Equal Protection Clause does not require absolute equality or precisely equal advantages. Nor, indeed, in view of the infinite variables affecting the educational process, can any system assure equal quality of education except in the most relative sense. Texas asserts that the Minimum Foundation Program provides an "adequate" education for all children in the State. By providing 12 years of free public-school education, and by assuring teachers, books, transportation, and operating funds, the Texas Legislature has endeavored to "guarantee, for the welfare of the state as a whole, that all people shall have at least an adequate program of education. This is what is meant by 'A Minimum Foundation Program of Education.' " The State repeatedly asserted in its briefs in this Court that it has fulfilled this desire and that it now assures "every child in every school district an adequate education." No proof was offered at trial persuasively discrediting or refuting the State's assertion.

For these two reasons—the absence of any evidence that the financing system discriminates against any definable category of "poor" people or that it results in the absolute deprivation of education—the disadvantaged class is not susceptible of identification in traditional terms. . . .

Education, of course, is not among the rights afforded explicit protection under our Federal Constitution. Nor do we find any basis for saying it is implicitly so protected. As we have said, the undisputed importance of education will not alone cause this Court to depart from the usual standard for reviewing a State's social and economic legislation. It is appellees' contention, however, that education is distinguishable from other services and benefits provided by the State because it bears a peculiarly close relationship to other rights and liberties accorded protection under the Constitution. Specifically, they insist that education is itself a fundamental personal right because it is essential to the effective exercise of First Amendment freedoms and to intelligent utilization of the right to vote. In asserting a nexus between speech and education, appellees urge that the right to speak is meaningless unless the speaker is capable of articulating his thoughts intelligently and persuasively. . . .

We have carefully considered each of the arguments supportive of the District Court's finding that education is a fundamental right or liberty and have found those arguments unpersuasive. . . .

It should be clear, for the reasons stated above and in accord with the prior decisions of this Court, that this is not a case in which challenged state action must be subjected to the searching judicial scrutiny reserved for laws that create suspect classifications or impinge upon constitutionally protected rights.

We need not rest our decision, however, solely on the inappropriateness of the strict-scrutiny test. A century of Supreme Court adjudication under the Equal Protection Clause affirmatively supports the application of the traditional standard of review, which requires only that the State's system be shown to bear some rational relationship to legitimate state purposes. This case represents far more than a challenge to the manner in which Texas provides for the education of its children. We have here nothing less than a direct attack on the way in which Texas has chosen to raise and disburse state and local tax revenues. . . .

Thus, we stand on familiar ground when we continue to acknowledge that the Justices of this Court lack both the expertise and the familiarity with local problems so necessary to the making of wise decisions with respect to the raising and disposition of public revenues. Yet, we are urged to direct the States either to alter drastically the present system or to throw out the property tax altogether in favor of some other form of taxation. No scheme of taxation, whether the tax is imposed on property, income, or purchases of goods and services, has yet been devised which is free of all discriminatory impact. In such a complex arena in which no perfect alternatives exist, the

Court does well not to impose too rigorous a standard of scrutiny lest all local fiscal schemes become subjects of criticism under the Equal Protection Clause. . . .

In sum, to the extent that the Texas system of school financing results in unequal expenditures between children who happen to reside in different districts, we cannot say that such disparities are the product of a system that is so irrational as to be invidiously discriminatory. Texas has acknowledged its shortcomings and has persistently endeavored—not without some success—to ameliorate the differences in levels of expenditures without sacrificing the benefits of local participation. The Texas plan is not the result of hurried, ill-conceived legislation. It certainly is not the product of purposeful discrimination against any group or class. On the contrary, it is rooted in decades of experience in Texas and elsewhere, and in major part is the product of responsible studies by qualified people. In giving substance to the presumption of validity to which the Texas system is entitled, *Lindsley v. Natural Carbonic Gas Co.*, 220 U.S. 61, 78 (1911), it is important to remember that at every stage of its development it has constituted a "rough accommodation" of interests in an effort to arrive at practical and workable solutions. *Metropolis Theatre Co. v. City of Chicago*, 228 U.S. 61, 69–70 (1913). One also must remember that the system here challenged is not peculiar to Texas or to any other State. In its essential characteristics, the Texas plan for financing public education reflects what many educators for a half century have thought was an enlightened approach to a problem for which there is no perfect solution. We are unwilling to assume for ourselves a level of wisdom superior to that of legislators, scholars, and educational authorities in 50 States, especially where the alternatives proposed are only recently conceived and nowhere yet tested. The constitutional standard under the Equal Protection Clause is whether the challenged state action rationally furthers a legitimate state purpose or interest. *McGinnis v. Royster*, 410 U.S. 263, 270 (1973). We hold that the Texas plan abundantly satisfies this standard.

**Concurring Opinion**   MR. JUSTICE STEWART, concurring.

The method of financing public schools in Texas, as in almost every other State, has resulted in a system of public education that can fairly be described as chaotic and unjust. It does not follow, however, and I cannot find, that this system violates the Constitution of the United States. I join the opinion and judgment of the Court because I am convinced that any other course would mark an extraordinary departure from principled adjudication under the Equal Protection Clause of the Fourteenth Amendment. The uncharted directions of such a departure are suggested, I think, by the imaginative dissenting opinion my Brother Marshall has filed today.

**Dissenting Opinion**    MR. JUSTICE MARSHALL, with whom MR. JUSTICE DOUGLAS concurs, dissenting.

To begin, I must once more voice my disagreement with the Court's rigidified approach to equal protection analysis. See *Dandridge v. Williams*, 397 U.S. 471, 519–521 (1970) (dissenting opinion); *Richardson v. Belcher*, 404 U.S. 78, 90 (1971) (dissenting opinion). The Court apparently seeks to establish today that equal protection cases fall into one of two neat categories which dictate the appropriate standard of review—strict scrutiny or mere rationality. But this Court's decisions in the field of equal protection defy such easy categorization. A principled reading of what this Court has done reveals that it has applied a spectrum of standards in reviewing discrimination allegedly violative of the Equal Protection Clause. This spectrum clearly comprehends variations in the degree of care with which the Court will scrutinize particular classifications, depending, I believe, on the constitutional and societal importance of the interest adversely affected and the recognized invidiousness of the basis upon which the particular classification is drawn. I find in fact that many of the Court's recent decisions embody the very sort of reasoned approach to equal protection analysis for which I previously argued—that is, an approach in which "concentration [is] placed upon the character of the classification in question, the relative importance to individuals in the class discriminated against of the governmental benefits that they do not receive, and the asserted state interests in support of the classification." *Dandridge v. Williams, supra*, at 520–521 (dissenting opinion). . . .

The majority is, of course, correct when it suggests that the process of determining which interests are fundamental is a difficult one. But I do not think the problem is insurmountable. And I certainly do not accept the view that the process need necessarily degenerate into an unprincipled, subjective "picking-and-choosing" between various interests or that it must involve this Court in creating "substantive constitutional rights in the name of guaranteeing equal protection of the laws," *ante*, at 33. Although not all fundamental interests are constitutionally guaranteed, the determination of which interests are fundamental should be firmly rooted in the text of the Constitution. The task in every case should be to determine the extent to which constitutionally guaranteed rights are dependent on interests not mentioned in the Constitution. . . .

In summary, it seems to me inescapably clear that this Court has consistently adjusted the care with which it will review state discrimination in light of the constitutional significance of the interests affected and the invidiousness of the particular classification. In the context of economic interests, we find that discriminatory state action is almost always sustained, for such interests are generally far removed from constitutional guarantees. Moreover, "[t]he extremes to which the Court has gone in dreaming up rational bases for state regulation in that area may in many instances be ascribed to a healthy revulsion from the Court's earlier excesses in using the Constitution to protect interests that have more than enough power to protect themselves in the legislative halls." *Dandridge v. Williams*, 397 U.S., at 520 (dissenting opinion). But the situation differs markedly when discrimination against important individual interests with constitutional implications and against particularly disadvantaged or powerless classes is involved. The majority suggests, however, that a variable standard of review would give this Court the appearance of a "super-legislature." *Ante*, at 31. I cannot agree. Such an approach seems to me a part of the guarantees of our Constitution and of the historic experiences with oppression of and discrimination against discrete, powerless minorities which underlie that document. In truth, the Court itself will be open to the criticism raised by the majority so long as it continues on its present course of effectively selecting in private which cases will be afforded special consideration without acknowledging the true basis of its action. . . .

## PLYLER v. DOE
### 457 U.S. 202 (1982)

JUSTICE BRENNAN delivered the opinion of the Court.

The question presented by these cases is whether, consistent with the Equal Protection Clause of the Fourteenth Amendment, Texas may deny to undocumented school-age children the free public education that it provides to children who are citizens of the United States or legally admitted aliens. . . .

The Equal Protection Clause directs that "all persons similarly circumstanced shall be treated alike." *F.S. Royster Guano Co. v. Virginia*, 253 U.S. 412, 415 (1920). But so too, "[t]he Constitution does not require things which are different in fact or opinion to be treated in law as though they were the same." *Tigner v. Texas*, 310 U.S. 141, 147 (1940). The initial discretion to determine what is "different" and what is "the same" resides in the legislatures of the States. A legislature must have substantial latitude to establish classifications that roughly approximate the nature of the problem perceived, that accommodate competing concerns both public and private, and that account for limitations on the practical ability of the State to remedy every ill. In applying the Equal Protection Clause to most forms of state action, we thus seek only the assurance that the classification at issue bears some fair relationship to a legitimate public purpose.

But we would not be faithful to our obligations under the Fourteenth Amendment if we applied so deferential a standard to every classification. The Equal Protection Clause was intended as a restriction on state legislative action inconsistent with elemental constitutional premises. Thus we have treated as presumptively invidious those classifications that disadvantage a "suspect class," or that impinge upon the exercise of a "fundamental right." With respect to such classifications, it is appropriate to enforce the mandate of equal protection by requiring the State to demonstrate that its classification has been precisely tailored to serve a compelling governmental interest. In addition, we have recognized that certain forms of legislative classification, while not facially invidious, nonetheless give rise to recurring constitutional difficulties; in these limited circumstances we have sought the assurance that the classification reflects a reasoned judgment consistent with the ideal of equal protection by inquiring whether it may fairly be viewed as furthering a substantial interest of the State. . . .

Sheer incapability or lax enforcement of the laws barring entry into this country, coupled with the failure to establish an effective bar to the employment of undocumented aliens, has resulted in the creation of a substantial "shadow population" of illegal migrants—numbering in the millions—within our borders. This situation raises the specter of a permanent caste of undocumented resident aliens, encouraged by some to remain here as a source of cheap labor, but nevertheless denied the benefits that our society makes available to citizens and lawful residents. The existence of such an underclass presents most difficult problems for a Nation that prides itself on adherence to principles of equality under law.

The children who are plaintiffs in these cases are special members of this underclass. Persuasive arguments support the view that a State may withhold its beneficence from those whose very presence within the United States is the product of their own unlawful conduct. These arguments do not apply with the same force to classifications imposing disabilities on the minor *children* of such illegal entrants. At the least, those who elect to enter our territory by stealth and in violation of our law should be prepared to bear the consequences, including, but not limited to, deportation. But the children of those illegal entrants are not comparably situated. Their "parents have the ability to conform their conduct to societal norms," and presumably the ability to remove themselves from the State's jurisdiction; but the children who are plaintiffs in these cases "can affect neither their parents' conduct nor their own status." *Trimble v. Gordon*, 430 U.S. 762, 770 (1977). Even if the State found it expedient to control the conduct of adults by acting against their children, legislation directing the onus of a parent's misconduct against his children does not comport with fundamental conceptions of justice. . . .

Of course, undocumented status is not irrelevant to any proper legislative goal. Nor is undocumented status an absolutely immutable characteristic since it is the product of conscious, indeed unlawful, action. But § 21.031 is directed against children, and imposes its discriminatory burden on the basis of a legal characteristic over which children can have little control. It is thus difficult to conceive of a rational justification for penalizing these children for their presence within the United States. Yet that appears to be precisely the effect of § 21.031.

Public education is not a "right" granted to individuals by the Constitution. *San Antonio Independent School Dist. v. Rodriguez*, 411 U.S. 1, 35 (1973). But neither is it merely some governmental "benefit" indistinguishable from other forms of social welfare legislation. Both the importance of education in maintaining our basic institutions, and the lasting impact of its deprivation on the life of the child, mark the distinction. . . .

In addition, education provides the basic tools by which individuals might lead economically productive lives to the benefit of us all. In sum, education has a fundamental role in maintaining the fabric of our society. We cannot ignore the significant social costs borne by our Nation when select groups are denied the means to absorb the values and skills upon which our social order rests.

In addition to the pivotal role of education in sustaining our political and cultural heritage, denial of education to some isolated group of children poses an affront to one of the goals of the Equal Protection Clause: the abolition of governmental barriers presenting unreasonable obstacles to advancement on the basis of individual merit. Paradoxically, by depriving the children of any disfavored group of an education, we foreclose the means by which that group might raise the level of esteem in which it is held by the majority. . . .

These well-settled principles allow us to determine the proper level of deference to be afforded § 21.031. Undocumented aliens cannot be treated as a suspect class because their presence in this country in violation of federal law is not a "constitutional irrelevancy." Nor is education a fundamental right; a State need not justify by compelling necessity every variation in the manner in which education is provided to its population. See *San Antonio Independent School Dist. v. Rodriguez, supra*, at 28–39. But more is involved in these cases than the abstract question whether § 21.031 discriminates against a suspect class, or whether education is a fundamental right. Section 21.031 imposes a lifetime hardship on a discrete class of children not accountable for their disabling status. The stigma of illiteracy will mark them for the rest of their lives. By denying these children a basic education, we deny them the ability to live within the structure of our civic institutions, and foreclose any realistic possibility that they will contribute in even the smallest way to the progress of our Nation. In determining the rationality of § 21.031, we may appropriately take into account its costs to the Nation and to innocent children who are its victims. In light of these countervailing costs, the discrimination contained in § 21.031 can hardly be considered rational unless it furthers some substantial goal of the State. . . .

Finally, appellants suggest that undocumented children are appropriately singled out because their unlawful presence within the United States renders them less likely than other children to remain within the boundaries of the State, and to put their education to productive social or political use within the State. Even assuming that such an interest is legitimate, it is an interest that is most difficult to qualify. The State has no assurance that any child, citizen or not, will employ the education provided by the State within the confines of the State's borders. In any event, the record is clear that many of the undocumented children disabled by this classification will remain in this country indefinitely, and that some will become lawful residents or citizens of the United States. It is difficult to understand precisely what the State hopes to achieve by promoting the creation and perpetuation of a subclass of illiterates within our boundaries, surely adding to the problems and costs of unemployment, welfare, and crime. It is thus clear that whatever savings might be achieved by denying these children an education, they are wholly insubstantial in light of the costs involved to these children, the State, and the Nation.

If the State is to deny a discrete group of innocent children the free public education that it offers to other children residing within its borders, that denial must be justified by a showing that it furthers some substantial state interest. No such showing was made here. Accordingly, the judgment of the Court of Appeals in each of these cases is

*Affirmed.*

## ...........................DISCUSSION QUESTIONS...........................

1. Can you imagine how the laws of the United States might be different if the Supreme Court had never forced states to redraw congressional district boundaries based on the census?

2. Do you think it is fair for the United States, with its Senate based on area rather than population, to tell the states they cannot have a Senate based on area?

3. In 1994 several states, including California and Florida, sued the federal government for billions of dollars to cover the cost of educating and caring for illegal immigrants. Do you think it is fair for the Supreme Court to force states to educate illegal aliens while the federal government refuses to help cover the cost of this education?

4. In November 1994, the people of California voted to deny education and most health care to illegal immigrants. Do you think this is constitutional in the wake of the Supreme Court ruling in *Plyer v. Doe*?

5. In what elections do you think it would be fair to allow only people with property to vote?

6. Critics from other societies find it difficult to understand that poor people in the United States have a right to a court-appointed attorney but do not have the right to eat or have a place to live. What would you say to this criticism? How does the history of the United States and its legal system make this result possible?

7. People in states such as Illinois and Georgia thought that people moving into the big cities in their states from other states were not "real" citizens of Illinois or Georgia. The people of Illinois objected to "southerners" moving into Chicago, while the people of Georgia objected that too many "Yankees" were moving into Atlanta. Do you think the authors of the Fourteenth Amendment would be pleased, or unhappy, that the amendment was ultimately interpreted in a way that brought an end to this kind of thinking, at least as far as the right to vote was concerned?

# CHAPTER
## eight

* * * * * * * *

# Equal Protection Today

While Supreme Court decisions in other areas of constitutional interpretation have certainly had an impact on American society, nothing compares with the impact of the Court's equal protection decisions. Imagine the United States in the 1950s. In large parts of the country, signs designated where black people could eat, drink from a water fountain, or sit in a theater. White children did not attend school with black children, even in the North. Poor people did not receive a court-appointed attorney and could not vote if they could not come up with the poll tax. Women were second-class citizens in many ways, kept from holding some jobs and serving on juries in some states. People living in large cities such as Chicago or Atlanta lived in states where a very small percentage of the population living in rural areas controlled the state legislature and the state budget. Urban dwellers in such states were second-class citizens, regardless of their race, sex, or class.

Looking back now, the United States in the 1950s almost seems like another world. It is hard to imagine what it must have been like when state governments took money out of large cities to provide services to rural areas even though the need in the cities was far greater; when race discrimination was open, obvious, and everywhere; when women were not allowed to have certain jobs because of their "special nature." Beginning with the 1954 decision in *Brown v. Board of Education*, the Supreme Court took the lead in addressing discrimination, eventually forcing the president and Congress to act. Chief Justice Earl Warren and the Warren Court, handing down decisions from 1953 to 1969, marked the real break with the past.

Of course, the Supreme Court did not bring about change alone. Congress passed a series of civil rights acts, and presidents enforced those laws and

Supreme Court decisions, in some cases with the use of federal troops and armed marshals.

While the Equal Protection Clause of the Fourteenth Amendment has brought about less discrimination against women, urban dwellers, and the poor, it is in the area of race discrimination that it has had its greatest impact. For almost a century, the United States did not keep the promise it made of equal protection under the laws to those who fought and died to bring about an end to slavery. It would require the passage of a century, two world wars, and major political upheaval before that promise would begin to be fulfilled.

## EQUAL PROTECTION ANALYSIS

Because of the difficulty in interpreting the Equal Protection Clause, the Court has developed a special kind of legal analysis to aid in this task. Beginning in the 1940s the Court developed the idea that there were two basic types of equal protection analysis. Discrimination based on race was subject to what the Court came to call "strict scrutiny," which meant that the discriminatory practice had to be balanced against the reason for the discrimination, and discrimination would only be allowed if the government had a "compelling reason." In the vast majority of cases, the reason was not found to be compelling enough to justify race discrimination. Every other kind of discrimination had to meet a "rationality" test. In applying the rationality test the Court asked whether the distinction drawn by the statute was "rational" and supported by any "reasonable" interest. Almost any reason was good enough.

Beginning in the 1950s the Court moved away from this approach toward an approach that asked two questions: What is the basis of the discrimination? What right or activity are the people who are being discriminated against being kept from enjoying? The Court developed what could be considered a sliding scale of analysis. The more "suspect" the basis of the discrimination, the "stricter" the analysis and the more "compelling" the reason for the discrimination had to be. Also, as the importance of the "right or privilege" that had been denied increased, the stricter the analysis became. This is presented graphically in Figure 1.1 (see p. 9).

At various times some members of the Court have argued that there are only two types of analysis: strict scrutiny and rationality. Over time most of these justices have come to recognize that the Court has indeed clearly engaged in a "sliding scale" analysis like the one depicted in Figure 1.1.

At the same time, in the area of equal protection more than any other, the Supreme Court justices have been engaged in the articulation of society's values. The members of the Court have examined particular instances of discrimination and in each case have made a determination as to whether or not the discrimination "bothers" them in some fundamental way. If it does, the law or practice at issue is overturned. If it does not, the law or practice is upheld. In the Court's decisions about equal protection, three values that appear to be dominant are the value of equality in the political process, the value of economic opportunity, and the belief that the sins of the ancestors should not be visited on their descendants. While some justices have objected that the process of applying values to particular situations is simply "result-oriented" decision making, it is a fact that the Supreme Court has engaged in value-based decision making on many occasions when cases have involved the issue of equal protection.

The one area where the Court, as well as society in general, has not been able to come up with a workable solution is in the area of ending discrimination in the public schools. In the 1990s it is almost as true as it was in the 1950s that the best predictor of the quality of public education people receive in the United States is the color of their skin. After all the social trauma of the 1960s and 1970s over school integration, society has very little to show for it in many parts of the country. In many schools white children still finish high school without ever having had a black child as a classmate. Whether federal programs designed to help bring about greater integration in housing will alter this pattern remains to be seen.

The one area where the Court has failed to provide reasonable guidelines for society is affirmative action. Because so many justices have had their own personal views about affirmative action, society is still waiting for clear guidance. The questions for the 1990s and beyond may well be: When should affirmative action plans come to an end? When is an organization integrated enough to no longer use quotas or view race or sex as a plus for applicants? When does a group achieve a high enough social status that it no longer deserves special treatment? Should affirmative action be available to everyone, even people who have just immigrated to the United States and whose ancestors never suffered in any way from past discrimination? Presumably, the Court will have to answer these and other questions in the years to come.

Looking back over the decades, one assumption made by the Court in the 1896 *Plessy* decision has clearly been demonstrated to have been wrong. In his decision for the majority, Justice Brown rejected the idea that "social prejudices may be overcome by legislation" or that the simple act of race separation "stamps the colored race with a badge of inferiority." Anyone who compares the United States in the 1950s with the United States in the 1990s knows that this was an erroneous assumption. While legislation may not, alone, overcome social prejudice, it can go a long way toward making prejudice illegitimate. Separation caused by law seems natural. Separation when it is no longer caused by law seems unnatural. Social integration, slow as it may be, can only proceed after legal segregation has ended.

When Americans declared their independence from England, they also declared their fundamental values. They held certain truths to be "self-evident," including

> all men are created equal, that they are endowed by their Creator with certain unalienable Rights, that among these are Life, Liberty and the pursuit of Happiness.

The United States has spent over two centuries trying to live up to these self-evident truths. On August 28, 1963, the Reverend Martin Luther King, Jr. invoked these words as he stood on the steps of the Lincoln Memorial and spoke to 250,000 people. He said that he had a dream that one day the United States would "live out the true meaning of this creed." He hoped that one day "the sons of slaves and the sons of former slaveowners" would be able to "sit down together at the table of brotherhood" and that one day the "jangling discord of our Nation" would be turned into "a beautiful symphony of brotherhood." While that day may not yet be upon us, the United States has certainly made progress. The goal that everyone should enjoy "the equal protection of the laws" is certainly much nearer than it was that day in 1963.

At the end of the Civil War a group of senators and representatives had a vision of a new America. These men are often referred to as "radical Republicans" in the history books. They imagined a society in which former slaves would own land and enjoy all the political and social rights of every other citizen. They imagined an America where race would no longer have a bearing on any aspect of life. They failed to turn their vision into reality. Too many forces were at work against them. The fact that they failed does not lessen the impact that their ideas would have on later generations. The names of these men are unknown to most Americans. Yet it was these men who added to the Constitution the most important phrase currently contained in that document, that all people should enjoy the "equal protection of the laws."

On July 2, 1863, the Union Army held the high ground at Gettysburg, Pennsylvania. The left flank of the Union line was on a hill called Little Round Top. A group of 300 soldiers from Maine held Little Round Top. Their orders were simple: they could do anything except retreat. In the course of fierce fighting, the soldiers from Maine finally ran out of ammunition. They then fixed bayonets and charged down the hill because retreat was not an option. They took the enemy by surprise and saved the day for the Union Army, which went on to win the battle, and ultimately the war. The United States of America has dedicated itself to three fundamental goals: liberty, democracy, and political equality. The goal of political equality proved to be the most difficult to achieve, but, throughout America's history, it was a goal from which retreat was not an option.

# GLOSSARY OF LEGAL TERMS

* * * * * * * * *

**A *fortiori*:** Latin, meaning literally "from the stronger." It is used by judges to mean that if one fact exists, another fact must follow from it. If someone is alive, then we know *a fortiori* that he or she is breathing.

**Allegation:** A statement of fact that has not yet been proven. In a criminal case we would say that allegations have been made against the defendant which the prosecutor will attempt to prove.

**Amicus curiae:** Latin, meaning literally "a friend of the Court." In some cases, especially in cases that have been appealed, other people besides those people directly involved in a case may have an interest in the outcome. In an effort to influence the justices, these people will file briefs as "friends of the Court," suggesting why the decision should come out one way or the other. When people file *amicus curiae* briefs, they are usually arguing that the court's decision will have an impact on them or on society in general which the court should consider when making its decision.

**Analogy:** A way of thinking about an issue that relates a particular situation to another situation by identifying similarities. People involved in a case often argue that their case is analogous (or similar) to another case because they know what the court decided in the other case and they would like the court to make the same decision in their case.

**Appeal:** A request to a higher court to review the decision of a lower court. When a trial is over, the losing party may appeal the decision to an appeals court.

**Appellant/Appellee:** The appellant is the person who appeals a case to a higher court; the appellee is the person who has to respond to the appeal.

**Atheist:** A person who does not believe in the existence of a God.

**Bill of attainder:** A law passed by a legislature declaring that a particular person or a group of persons is guilty of a crime. The person, or group of persons, to whom the bill of attainder applies has not received a trial.

**Brief:** A written document given to a judge to support a particular legal opinion. When a case is appealed to a higher court, each side will file a brief explaining why it should win the case. Other people may also file briefs as "friends of the Court" (*amicus curiae* briefs), pointing out the effects a decision may have on them or on society in general.

**Certiorari:** Latin, meaning literally "to be certain." In American law, when someone wants to appeal his or her case to the U.S. Supreme Court, he or she usually asks for a writ of certiorari. If the Court agrees to hear the case, it issues a writ of certiorari which orders the parties in the case to bring the case before the court.

**Circuit Court of Appeals:** In the federal judicial system, the district court conducts the trial and the Supreme Court hears cases on appeal. There is an appeals court between the district court and the Supreme Court, called the circuit court. Generally a case must be appealed to the circuit court before it can go on to the Supreme Court.

**Citizen:** Someone who is a full legal member of a nation. In the United States, only a citizen can vote and hold some public offices.

**Civil:** In American law, most cases are either civil or criminal. In a civil case, one person sues another person. In a criminal case, the government claims that someone has broken the law and should pay a fine or go to jail.

**Common law:** Common law is law made by judges as opposed to statutes passed by legislatures. In ancient times, people were subject to the laws of their tribe. After his conquest of England in 1066 A.D., William I decided that there should be one law for all of the subjects in his kingdom. This law was developed mainly by the king's judges, as they made decisions and then based later decisions on their decisions in earlier cases. Over the centuries the English judges developed many legal principles that became the basis for most of their decisions in civil cases. These principles became the common law for England and her colonies. The United States inherited this common law. It has been modified by the judges in each state over the centuries, so that today each state is considered to have its own unique common law. The main exception to this is Louisiana, which bases its law on French and Spanish law, not the English common law.

**Conscientious objector:** A person who, for reasons of conscience, objects to fighting in a war. To qualify as a true "conscientious objector," the person must believe that war is objectionable in general, and not just object to a particular war.

**Constitution:** In the United States, the Constitution is a written document that forms the supreme law and organization of the government. Governments may exercise only those powers granted to them by the Constitution and they are limited by the rights reserved for the individual citizens.

**Criminal:** *See* **Civil.**

*De minimis:* The short form of the Latin phrase *de minimis non curat lex*, which means the law does not care about very "minimal" or small things. If a legal violation is technically a violation of the law but so small as to be not worth the court's time, the judge may dismiss the case as *de minimis.*

**Defendant:** A defendant is someone who is being sued or is charged with committing a crime.

**Dicta:** From the Latin, meaning statements of opinion by a judge that are not directly relevant to the decision of the case. Dicta are general statements concerning a particular judge's definition of the law but that do not directly relate to the case before the court.

**Dissent:** When a group of judges is making a decision and some of the judges do not agree with the majority, they will "dissent" from the majority opinion. To dissent simply means to disagree. They may state their dissent, or they may write a dissenting opinion explaining why they disagree. On some occasions a dissenting opinion has convinced the group to reverse its opinion about a decision.

**District court:** In the federal judicial system, trial of a case is held at the district court. A case may then be appealed to the circuit court, and from there to the Supreme Court. It is the district court that determines the facts of the case.

**Ex post facto law:** A law passed after an act has been committed. Conviction on the basis of an ex post facto law is not allowed in the United States; a person may only be convicted of acts for which laws were actually on the books when the act was committed.

**Holding:** The decision of the court and the reason for that decision. Attorneys generally say that the holding of the case is the reason why the winning party in a case was successful.

**Impeachment:** Impeachment occurs when a public official is removed from office for having done something illegal or immoral.

*In loco parentis:* Latin, meaning literally "in the place of the parent." *In loco parentis* is a legal concept that says that if someone, such as a babysitter or a teacher, has been put in charge of a child, then that person has the same power over the child that the child's parent would have.

*Infra:* Latin, meaning literally "below." If a judge mentions a case briefly that he or she will be discussing in detail later in the decision, then the judge may put the word *infra* after the name of the case. This lets the reader know that the case will be discussed later in more detail.

**Injunction:** A court order telling a person to do, or not to do, something. People might say that a person has been "injoined" from acting. A restraining order is one kind of injunction.

**Interstate commerce:** The movement of goods across state lines in the United States. Under the U.S. Constitution, the federal government is given the power to control "interstate commerce" to make sure that goods flow between states with a minimum of disruption.

**Jurisdiction:** The area over which a particular court has power. For example, the U.S. Supreme Court can only decide cases concerned with federal law and questions of constitutional interpretation. Most issues are within the jurisdiction of state courts, not federal courts.

**Mens rea:** Latin, meaning literally "guilty mind." Generally, a person cannot be found guilty of a crime unless he or she had a "guilty mind," meaning he or she intended to do harm or to commit a crime.

**Naturalization:** The process by which a noncitizen becomes a citizen.

*Parens patriae:* Latin, meaning literally "the parent of the country." In ancient times this term meant that the king was regarded as the ultimate parent for everyone and had the power to act as the parent of any subject in the kingdom if the subject's real parents were not available. In countries without a king, the term means that, if there is no natural parent to deal with a problem, then the government may have to fulfill that function. For example, the government may act as a parent in dealing with a child, with an insane person, or with someone who is not capable of dealing with things for himself or herself.

**Per curiam:** Latin, meaning literally "by the court." When an opinion has been written by the court as a whole, rather than by one particular judge, it is called a *per curiam* decision.

**Petitioner:** A person who petitions a judge to make a decision. Someone who files a lawsuit or begins an appeal can be called a petitioner. The person who is being sued or is defending against an appeal is the respondent.

**Plaintiff:** In a lawsuit, the person who brings the lawsuit is called the plaintiff. The person being sued by the plaintiff is called the defendant. The defendant defends against the charges that have been brought by the plaintiff.

**Police power:** A concept of U.S. law. Courts in the United States have decided that state constitutions provide state governments with police power, meaning the power to do everything that it is "reasonable" for government to do. Although the U.S. Constitution spells out the powers of the federal government, most state constitutions do not do this. The police power is very broad and includes the power to build roads, fight disease, and put people in jail; however, a court can decide that a particular action by a state legislature is unconstitutional if it is beyond the police power. The problem with this broad concept is that it is very vague and gives courts a great deal of power to declare the actions of legislatures to be unconstitutional as a violation of the state constitution. If a state government takes action beyond its power, the court does not have to ask whether or not any rights protected by the Bill of Rights have been violated. A court may invalidate an action of government either because the action was beyond the power of government or because it violated a right protected by the Bill of Rights.

**Precedent:** In the U.S. legal system, lower courts are bound by the decisions of courts above them. We say that those higher court decisions serve as precedents for the decisions to be made by the lower courts.

**Restraining order:** A court order that orders someone not to do something. If a person wants to stop another person from doing something, he or she may ask a judge for a restraining order against that other person.

**Scienter:** Latin, meaning "knowingly." Generally people cannot be convicted of crimes unless they acted knowingly, with scienter, meaning that the people knew what they were doing when they committed the crime. They were not acting unconsciously or without knowledge of the facts in the case.

**Separation of powers:** Generally government is thought of as having three basic powers: the power to make the law (legislative), the power to enforce the law (executive), and the power to decide what the law is (judicial). In the

United States, these three powers are separate from each other. That has not always been true in other countries or in the past. In ancient Athens, for example, the legislature was also the supreme court.

**Standing:** In the American legal system, people are generally not allowed to complain about a violation of the law or the Constitution unless the violation has injured them personally in some way. Only people who actually have been injured have standing to complain about their injury in a civil or criminal case.

*Stare decisis:* Latin, meaning literally "the decision must stand." In American law, once a particular court has made a decision, it is expected that the court will not change its ruling. People can then alter their behavior to comply with the decision without fear that it will change in the near future. This concept is particularly important for the U.S. Supreme Court because Supreme Court decisions have such a far-reaching impact on society.

**Statute:** A law passed by a legislative body, such as a state legislature or the U.S. Congress.

**Stipulate:** The purpose of a trial is to determine the facts of a particular case. If there are facts on which both sides agree, then both sides will "stipulate" that those facts are true and correct. For the rest of the trial, everyone will assume that those facts are true without having to prove them.

*Supra:* Latin, meaning literally "above." If a judge has already discussed a case in detail and wishes to mention it briefly again, he or she may put the word *supra* after the name of the case to let the reader know that the case has already been discussed in detail earlier in the decision.

**Tort:** Comes from the same Latin root as words such as *twist* and *torture*. In American law, if one person has injured another person in some way, we say that a tort has been committed. The injury may be physical, economic, or psychological. When people sue because they have been injured, we say they are "suing in tort."

**Ubiquity:** The concept that something can be everywhere at the same time, omnipresent. Some believe that God is ubiquitous. We generally conceive that the law and government are ubiquitous, even if there is no government official at a particular place at a particular time.

**Writ of habeas corpus:** A court order that requires a person who has someone under custody to either bring that person to court or release him or her from custody.

# FURTHER READING

※ ※ ※ ※ ※ ※ ※ ※

Altschiller, Donald, ed. *Affirmative Action*. New York: H.W. Wilson Co., 1991.
   A collection of essays on all aspects of affirmative action.

Asch, Sidney. *Civil Rights and Responsibilities under the Constitution*. New York: Arco, 1968.
   Discusses the conflict between majority rule and minority rights.

Bell, Derrick A. *Race, Racism & American Law*. Boston, MA: Little, Brown & Co., 1980.
   Examines issues of race in American law.

Bickel, Alexander M. *The Morality of Consent*. New Haven, CT: Yale University Press, 1975.
   Explores the impact of political philosophers on interpretations of the Constitution.

Crist, Ray C. *The Invisible Children*. Cambridge, MA: Harvard University Press, 1978.
   Discusses the problem of integration in public schools.

Edsall, Thomas Byrne. *The New Politics of Inequality*. New York: W.W. Norton & Co., 1984.
   Argues that the rich have taken over politics in Washington, DC, to the detriment of the poor and the middle class.

Fehrenbacher, Don E. *The Dred Scott Case*. New York: Oxford University Press, 1978.
   Discusses the significance of the *Dred Scott* case in the history of American law and politics.

Forer, Lois G. *Money and Justice: Who Owns the Courts?* New York: W.W. Norton & Co., 1987.
   Asserts that justice is only for the rich.

Formisano, Ronald P. *Boston against Busing*. Chapel Hill, NC: University of North Carolina Press, 1991.
> Examines the fight over forced busing to achieve racial integration in the Boston public schools.

Garrow, David J. *Protest at Selma*. New Haven, CT: Yale University Press, 1978.
> Traces events that led up to the passage of the Voting Rights Act and what happened after it was passed.

Gillette, William. *The Right to Vote*. Baltimore, MD: Johns Hopkins University Press, 1967.
> Discusses the politics involved in the passage of the Fifteenth Amendment.

Harr, Charles Monroe, and Fessler, Daniel William. *The Wrong Side of the Tracks*. New York: Simon & Schuster, 1986.
> Looks at the role the common law can play in bringing about equal protection of the law for the poor.

Levine, Donald M., and Bane, Mary Jo. *The Inequality Controversy*. New York: Basic Books, 1975.
> A collection of essays on racial integration in the public schools.

McPherson, James M. *What They Fought For, 1861-1865*. Baton Rouge, LA: Louisiana State University Press, 1994.
> Explores the reasons soldiers on both sides fought in the Civil War as expressed in their letters.

Nelson, William E. *The Fourteenth Amendment*. Cambridge, MA: Harvard University Press, 1988.
> Examines the goals of the authors of the Fourteenth Amendment and the Supreme Court's interpretation of the amendment.

Orfield, Gary. *Must We Bus? Segregated Schools & National Policy*. Washington, DC: Brookings Institution, 1978.
> Argues that busing was necessary to integrate public schools in the United States.

Pole, J. R. *The Pursuit of Equality in American History*. Berkeley, CA: University of California Press, 1978.
> Traces the evolution of the idea of political equality through American history.

Rhode, Deborah L. *Justice & Gender*. Cambridge, MA: Harvard University Press, 1989.
> Reviews sex discrimination laws in the United States.

Ryan, William. *Equality*. New York: Pantheon Books, 1981.
> Discusses the basic foundations of inequality in American social thought.

Schwartz, Bernard, ed. *The Fourteenth Amendment*. New York: New York University Press, 1970.
> A collection of essays about the Fourteenth Amendment on the occasion of its 100th birthday.

Sickels, Robert J. *Race, Marriage and the Law*. Albuquerque, NM: University of New Mexico Press, 1972.

Examines the case of *Loving v. Virginia*, which declared laws against interracial marriage to be unconstitutional.

Steiner, Gilbert Y. *Constitutional Inequality*. Washington, DC: The Brookings Institution, 1985.

Discusses why the ERA (the Equal Rights Amendment for women) failed to be ratified.

Whalen, Charles, and Whalen, Barbara. *The Longest Debate*. Cabin John, MD: Seven Locks Press, 1985.

Presents the history of the 1964 Civil Rights Act.

# APPENDIX A

❋ ❋ ❋ ❋ ❋ ❋ ❋ ❋

# Constitution of the United States

## PREAMBLE

We the People of the United States, in Order to form a more perfect Union, establish Justice, insure domestic Tranquility, provide for the common defence, promote the general Welfare, and secure the Blessings of Liberty to ourselves and our Posterity, do ordain and establish this Constitution for the United States of America.

## ARTICLE I

*Section 1.* All legislative Powers herein granted shall be vested in a Congress of the United States, which shall consist of a Senate and House of Representatives.

*Section 2.* The House of Representatives shall be composed of Members chosen every second Year by the People of the several States, and the Electors in each State shall have the Qualifications requisite for Electors of the most numerous Branch of the State Legislature.

No Person shall be a Representative who shall not have attained to the age of twenty five Years, and been seven Years a Citizen of the United States, and who shall not, when elected, be an Inhabitant of that State in which he shall be chosen.

Representatives and direct Taxes shall be apportioned among the several States which may be included within this Union, according to their respective Numbers, which shall be determined by adding to the whole Number of free Persons, including those bound to Service for a Term of Years, and excluding Indians not taxed, three fifths of all other Persons. The actual

Enumeration shall be made within three Years after the first Meeting of the Congress of the United States, and within every subsequent Term of ten Years, in such Manner as they shall by Law direct. The Number of Representatives shall not exceed one for every thirty Thousand, but each State shall have at Least one Representative; and until such enumeration shall be made, the State of New Hampshire shall be entitled to chuse three, Massachusetts eight, Rhode-Island and Providence Plantations one, Connecticut five, New-York six, New Jersey four, Pennsylvania eight, Delaware one, Maryland six, Virginia ten, North Carolina five, South Carolina five, and Georgia three.

When vacancies happen in the Representation from any State, the Executive Authority thereof shall issue Writs of Election to fill such Vacancies.

The House of Representatives shall chuse their Speaker and other Officers; and shall have the sole Power of Impeachment.

*Section 3.* The Senate of the United States shall be composed of two Senators from each State, chosen by the Legislature thereof, for six Years; and each Senator shall have one Vote.

Immediately after they shall be assembled in Consequence of the first Election, they shall be divided as equally as may be into three Classes. The Seats of the Senators of the first Class shall be vacated at the Expiration of the second Year, of the second Class at the Expiration of the fourth Year, and of the third Class at the Expiration of the sixth Year, so that one third may be chosen every second Year; and if Vacancies happen by Resignation, or otherwise, during the Recess of the Legislature of any State, the Executive thereof may make temporary Appointments until the next Meeting of the Legislature, which shall then fill such Vacancies.

No Person shall be a Senator who shall not have attained to the Age of thirty Years, and been nine Years a Citizen of the United States, and who shall not, when elected, be an Inhabitant of that State for which he shall be chosen.

The Vice President of the United States shall be President of the Senate, but shall have no Vote, unless they be equally divided.

The Senate shall chuse their other Officers, and also a President pro tempore, in the Absence of the Vice President, or when he shall exercise the Office of President of the United States.

The Senate shall have the sole Power to try all Impeachments. When sitting for that Purpose, they shall be on Oath or Affirmation. When the President of the United States is tried the Chief Justice shall preside: And no Person shall be convicted without the Concurrence of two thirds of the Members present.

Judgment in Cases of Impeachment shall not extend further than to removal from Office, and disqualification to hold and enjoy any Office of honor, Trust or Profit under the United States: but the Party convicted shall nevertheless be liable and subject to Indictment, Trial, Judgment and Punishment, according to Law.

Section 4. The Times, Places and Manner of holding Elections for Senators and Representatives, shall be prescribed in each State by the Legislature thereof; but the Congress may at any time by Law make or alter such Regulations, except as to the Places of chusing Senators.

The Congress shall assemble at least once in every Year, and such Meeting shall be on the first Monday in December, unless they shall by Law appoint a different Day.

Section 5. Each House shall be the Judge of the Elections, Returns and Qualifications of its own Members, and a Majority of each shall constitute a Quorum to do Business; but a smaller Number may adjourn from day to day, and may be authorized to compel the Attendance of absent Members, in such Manner, and under such Penalties as each House may provide.

Each House may determine the Rules of its Proceedings, punish its Members for disorderly Behaviour, and, with the Concurrence of two thirds, expel a Member.

Each House shall keep a Journal of its Proceedings, and from time to time publish the same, excepting such Parts as may in their Judgment require Secrecy; and the Yeas and Nays of the Members of either House on any question shall, at the Desire of one fifth of those Present, be entered on the Journal.

Neither House, during the Session of Congress, shall, without the Consent of the other, adjourn for more than three days, nor to any other Place than that in which the two Houses shall be sitting.

Section 6. The Senators and Representatives shall receive a Compensation for their Services, to be ascertained by Law, and paid out of the Treasury of the United States. They shall in all Cases, except Treason, Felony and Breach of the Peace, be privileged from Arrest during their Attendance at the Session of their respective Houses, and in going to and returning from the same; and for any Speech or Debate in either House, they shall not be questioned in any other Place.

No Senator or Representative shall, during the Time for which he was elected, be appointed to any civil Office under the Authority of the United States, which shall have been created, or the Emoluments whereof shall have been encreased during such time; and no Person holding any Office under the United States, shall be a Member of either House during his Continuance in Office.

*Section 7.* All Bills for raising Revenue shall originate in the House of Representatives; but the Senate may propose or concur with amendments as on other Bills.

Every Bill which shall have passed the House of Representatives and the Senate, shall, before it become a Law, be presented to the President of the United States; If he approve he shall sign it, but if not he shall return it, with his Objections to that House in which it shall have originated, who shall enter the Objections at large on their Journal, and proceed to reconsider it. If after such Reconsideration two thirds of that House shall agree to pass the Bill, it shall be sent, together with the Objections, to the other House, by which it shall likewise be reconsidered, and if approved by two thirds of that House, it shall become a Law. But in all such Cases the Votes of both Houses shall be determined by yeas and Nays, and the Names of the Persons voting for and against the Bill shall be entered on the Journal of each House respectively. If any Bill shall not be returned by the President within ten Days (Sunday excepted) after it shall have been presented to him, the Same shall be a Law, in like Manner as if he had signed it, unless the Congress by their Adjournment prevent its Return, in which Case it shall not be a Law.

Every Order, Resolution, or Vote to which the Concurrence of the Senate and House of Representatives may be necessary (except on a question of Adjournment) shall be presented to the President of the United States; and before the Same shall take Effect, shall be approved by him, or being disapproved by him, shall be repassed by two thirds of the Senate and House of Representatives, according to the Rules and Limitations prescribed in the Case of a Bill.

*Section 8.* The Congress shall have Power To lay and collect Taxes, Duties, Imposts and Excises, to pay the Debts and provide for the common Defence and general Welfare of the United States; but all Duties, Imposts and Excises shall be uniform throughout the United States;

To borrow Money on the credit of the United States;

To regulate Commerce with foreign Nations, and among the several States, and with the Indian Tribes;

To establish an uniform Rule of Naturalization, and uniform Laws on the subject of Bankruptcies throughout the United States;

To coin Money, regulate the Value thereof, and of foreign Coin, and fix the Standard of Weights and Measures;

To provide for the Punishment of counterfeiting the Securities and current Coin of the United States;

To establish Post Offices and post Roads;

To promote the Progress of Science and useful Arts, by securing for limited Times to Authors and Inventors the exclusive Right to their respective Writings and Discoveries;

To constitute Tribunals inferior to the supreme Court;

To define and punish Piracies and Felonies commit[t]ed on the high Seas, and Offences against the Law of Nations;

To declare War, grant Letters of Marque and Reprisal, and make Rules concerning Captures on Land and Water;

To raise and support Armies, but no Appropriation of Money to that Use shall be for a longer Term than two Years;

To provide and maintain a Navy;

To make Rules for the Government and Regulation of the land and naval Forces;

To provide for calling forth the Militia to execute the Laws of the Union, suppress Insurrections and repel Invasions;

To provide for organizing, arming, and disciplining the Militia, and for governing such Part of them as may be employed in the Service of the United States, reserving to the States respectively, the Appointment of the Officers, and the Authority of training the Militia according to the discipline pre-scribed by Congress;

To exercise exclusive Legislation in all Cases whatsoever, over such District (not exceeding ten Miles square) as may, by Cession of Particular States, and the Acceptance of Congress, become the Seat of the Govern-ment of the United States, and to exercise like Authority over all Places purchased by the Consent of the Legislature of the State in which the Same shall be, for the Erection of Forts, Magazines, Arsenals, dock-Yards, and other needful Buildings;

—And

To make all Laws which shall be necessary and proper for carrying into Execution the foregoing Powers, and all other Powers vested by this Consti-tution in the Government of the United States, or in any Department or Officer thereof.

*Section 9.* The Migration or Importation of such Persons as any of the States now existing shall think proper to admit, shall not be prohibited by the Congress prior to the Year one thousand eight hundred and eight, but a Tax or duty may be imposed on such Importation, not exceeding ten dollars for each Person.

The Privilege of the Writ of Habeas Corpus shall not be suspended, unless when in Cases of Rebellion or Invasion the public Safety may require it.

No Bill of Attainder or ex post facto Law shall be passed.

No capitation, or other direct, Tax shall be laid, unless in Proportion to the Census or Enumeration herein before directed to be taken.

No Tax or Duty shall be laid on Articles exported from any State.

No Preference shall be given by any Regulation of Commerce or Revenue to the Ports of one State over those of another; nor shall Vessels bound to, or from, one State, be obliged to enter, clear or pay Duties in another.

No Money shall be drawn from the Treasury, but in Consequence of Appropriations made by Law; and a regular Statement and Account of the Receipts and Expenditures of all public Money shall be published from time to time.

No Title of Nobility shall be granted by the United States: And no Person holding any Office of Profit or Trust under them, shall, without the Consent of the Congress, accept of any present, Emolument, Office, or Title, of any kind whatever, from any King, Prince or foreign State.

*Section 10.* No State shall enter into any Treaty, Alliance, or Confederation; grant Letters of Marque and Reprisal; coin Money; emit Bills of Credit; make any Thing but gold and silver Coin a Tender in Payment of Debts; pass any Bill of Attainder, ex post facto Law, or Law impairing the Obligation of Contracts, or grant any Title of Nobility.

No State shall, without the Consent of the Congress, lay any Imposts or Duties on Imports or Exports, except what may be absolutely necessary for executing it's inspection Laws: and the net Produce of all Duties and Imposts, laid by any State on Imports or Exports, shall be for the Use of the Treasury of the United States; and all such Laws shall be subject to the Revision and Controul of the Congress.

No State shall, without the Consent of Congress, lay any Duty of Tonnage, keep Troops, or Ships of War in time of Peace, enter into any Agreement or Compact with another State, or with a foreign Power, or engage in War, unless actually invaded, or in such imminent Danger as will not admit of delay.

## ARTICLE II

*Section 1.* The executive Power shall be vested in a President of the United States of America. He shall hold his Office during the Term of four Years, and, together with the Vice President, chosen for the same Term, be elected, as follows.

Each State shall appoint, in such Manner as the Legislature thereof may direct, a Number of Electors, equal to the whole Number of Senators and Representatives to which the State may be entitled in the Congress: but no

Senator or Representative, or Person holding an Office of Trust or Profit under the United States, shall be appointed an Elector.

The Electors shall meet in their respective States, and vote by Ballot for two Persons, of whom one at least shall not be an Inhabitant of the same State with themselves. And they shall make a List of all the Persons voted for, and of the Number of Votes for each; which List they shall sign and certify, and transmit sealed to the Seat of the Government of the United States, directed to the President of the Senate. The President of the Senate shall, in the Presence of the Senate and House of Representatives, open all the Certificates, and the Votes shall then be counted. The Person having the greatest Number of Votes shall be the President, if such Number be a Majority of the whole Number of Electors appointed; and if there be more than one who have such Majority, and have an equal Number of Votes, then the House of Representatives shall immediately chuse by Ballot one of them for President; and if no Person have a Majority, then from the five highest on the list the said House shall in like Manner chuse the President. But in chusing the President, the Votes shall be taken by States, the Representation from each State having one Vote; a quorum for this Purpose shall consist of a Member or Members from two thirds of the States, and a Majority of all the States shall be necessary to a Choice. In every Case, after the Choice of the President, the Person having the greatest Number of Votes of the Electors shall be the Vice President. But if there should remain two or more who have equal Votes, the Senate shall chuse from them by Ballot the Vice President.

The Congress may determine the Time of chusing the Electors, and the Day on which they shall give their Votes; which Day shall be the same throughout the United States.

No Person except a natural born Citizen, or a Citizen of the United States, at the time of the Adoption of this Constitution, shall be eligible to the Office of President; neither shall any Person be eligible to that Office who shall not have attained to the Age of thirty five Years, and been fourteen Years a Resident within the United States.

In Case of the Removal of the President from Office, or of his Death, Resignation, or Inability to discharge the Powers and Duties of the said Office, the Same shall devolve on the Vice President, and the Congress may by Law provide for the Case of Removal, Death, Resignation or Inability, both of the President and Vice President, declaring what Officer shall then act as President, and such Officer shall act accordingly, until the Disability be removed, or a President shall be elected.

The President shall, at stated Times, receive for his Services, a Compensation, which shall neither be encreased nor diminished during the Period for which he shall have been elected, and he shall not receive within that Period any other Emolument from the United States, or any of them.

Before he enter on the Execution of his Office, he shall take the following Oath or Affirmation:—"I do solemnly swear (or affirm) that I will faithfully execute the Office of President of the United States, and will to the best of my Ability, preserve, protect and defend the Constitution of the United States."

*Section 2.* The President shall be Commander in Chief of the Army and Navy of the United States, and of the Militia of the several States, when called into the actual Service of the United States; he may require the Opinion, in writing, of the principal Officer in each of the executive Departments, upon any Subject relating to the Duties of their respective Offices, and he shall have Power to grant Reprieves and Pardons for Offenses against the United States, except in Cases of Impeachment.

He shall have Power, by and with the Advice and Consent of the Senate, to make Treaties, provided two thirds of the Senators present concur; and he shall nominate, and by and with the Advice and Consent of the Senate, shall appoint Ambassadors, other public Ministers and Consuls, Judges of the supreme Court, and all other Officers of the United States, whose Appointments are not herein otherwise provided for, and which shall be established by Law: but the Congress may by Law vest the Appointment of such inferior Officers, as they think proper, in the President alone, in the Courts of Law, or in the Heads of Departments.

The President shall have Power to fill up all Vacancies that may happen during the Recess of the Senate, by granting Commissions which shall expire at the End of their next Session.

*Section 3.* He shall from time to time give to the Congress Information of the State of the Union, and recommend to their Consideration such Measures as he shall judge necessary and expedient; he may, on extraordinary Occasions, convene both Houses, or either of them, and in Case of Disagreement between them, with Respect to the Time of Adjournment, he may adjourn them to such Time as he shall think proper; he shall receive Ambassadors and other public Ministers; he shall take Care that the Laws be faithfully executed, and shall Commission all the Officers of the United States.

*Section 4.* The President, Vice President and all Civil Officers of the United States, shall be removed from office on Impeachment for, and Conviction of, Treason, Bribery, or other high Crimes and Misdemeanors.

## ARTICLE III

*Section 1.* The judicial Power of the United States shall be vested in one supreme Court, and in such inferior Courts as the Congress may from time to time ordain and establish. The Judges, both of the supreme and inferior Courts, shall hold their Offices during good Behaviour, and shall, at stated Times, receive for their Services, a Compensation, which shall not be diminished during their Continuance in Office.

*Section 2.* The judicial Power shall extend to all Cases, in Law and Equity, arising under this Constitution, the Laws of the United States, and Treaties made, or which shall be made, under their Authority;—to all Cases affecting Ambassadors, other public Ministers and Consuls;—to all Cases of admiralty and maritime Jurisdiction;—to Controversies to which the United States shall be a Party;—to Controversies between two or more States;—between a State and Citizens of another State;—between Citizens of different States;—between Citizens of the same State claiming Lands under Grants of different States, and between a State, or the Citizens thereof, and foreign States, Citizens or Subjects.

In all Cases affecting Ambassadors, other public Ministers and Consuls, and those in which a State shall be Party, the supreme Court shall have original Jurisdiction. In all the other Cases before mentioned, the supreme Court shall have appellate Jurisdiction, both as to Law and Fact, with such Exceptions, and under such Regulations as the Congress shall make.

The Trial of all Crimes, except in cases of Impeachment, shall be by Jury; and such Trial shall be held in the State where the said Crimes shall have been committed; but when not committed within any State, the Trial shall be at such Place or Places as the Congress may by Law have directed.

*Section 3.* Treason against the United States shall consist only in levying War against them, or in adhering to their Enemies, giving them Aid and Comfort. No Person shall be convicted of Treason unless on the Testimony of two Witnesses to the same overt Act, or on Confession in open Court.

The Congress shall have Power to declare the Punishment of Treason, but no Attainder of Treason shall work Corruption of Blood, or Forfeiture except during the Life of the Person attainted.

## ARTICLE IV

*Section 1.* Full Faith and Credit shall be given in each State to the public Acts, Records, and judicial Proceedings of every other State. And the Congress may by general Laws prescribe the Manner in which such Acts, Records and Proceedings shall be proved, and the Effect thereof.

*Section 2.* The Citizens of each State shall be entitled to all Privileges and Immunities of Citizens in the several States.

A Person charged in any State with Treason, Felony, or other Crime, who shall flee from Justice, and be found in another State, shall on Demand of the executive Authority of the State from which he fled, be delivered up, to be removed to the State having Jurisdiction of the Crime.

No Person held to Service or Labour in one State, under the Laws thereof, escaping into another, shall, in Consequence of any Law or Regulation therein, be discharged from such Service or Labour, but shall be delivered up on Claim of the Party to whom such Service or Labour may be due.

*Section 3.* New States may be admitted by the Congress into this Union; but no new State shall be formed or erected within the Jurisdiction of any other State; nor any State be formed by the Junction of two or more States, or Parts of States, without the Consent of the Legislatures of the States concerned as well as of the Congress.

The Congress shall have Power to dispose of and make all needful Rules and Regulations respecting the Territory or other Property belonging to the United States; and nothing in this Constitution shall be so construed as to Prejudice any Claims of the United States, or of any particular State.

*Section 4.* The United States shall guarantee to every State in this Union a Republican Form of Government, and shall protect each of them against invasion; and on Application of the Legislature, or of the Executive (when the Legislature cannot be convened) against domestic Violence.

## ARTICLE V

The Congress, whenever two thirds of both Houses shall deem it necessary, shall propose Amendments to this Constitution, or, on the Application of the Legislatures of two thirds of the several States, shall call a Convention for proposing Amendments, which, in either Case, shall be valid to all Intents and Purposes, as Part of this Constitution, when ratified by the Legislatures of three fourths of the several States, or by Conventions in three fourths thereof, as the one or the other Mode of Ratification may be proposed by the Congress; Provided that no Amendment which may be made prior to the Year One thousand eight hundred and eight shall in any Manner affect the first and fourth Clauses in the Ninth Section of the first Article; and that no State, without its Consent, shall be deprived of its equal Suffrage in the Senate.

## ARTICLE VI

All Debts contracted and Engagements entered into, before the Adoption of this Constitution, shall be as valid against the United States under this Constitution, as under the Confederation.

This Constitution, and the Laws of the United States which shall be made in Pursuance thereof; and all Treaties made, or which shall be made, under the Authority of the United States, shall be the supreme Law of the Land; and the Judges in every State shall be the supreme Law of the Land; and the Judges in every State shall be bound thereby, any Thing in the Constitution or Laws of any State to the Contrary notwithstanding.

The Senators and Representatives before mentioned, and the Members of the several State Legislatures, and all executive and judicial Officers, both of the United States and of the several States, shall be bound by Oath or Affirmation, to support this Constitution; but no religious Test shall ever be required as a Qualification to any Office or public Trust under the United States.

## ARTICLE VII

The Ratification of the Conventions of nine States, shall be sufficient for the Establishment of this Constitution between the States so ratifying the Same.

## AMENDMENTS

### Amendment I

Congress shall make no law respecting an establishment of religion, or prohibiting the free exercise thereof; or abridging the freedom of speech, or of the press; or the right of the people peaceably to assemble, and to petition the Government for a redress of grievances.

### Amendment II

A well regulated Militia, being necessary to the security of a free State, the right of the people to keep and bear Arms, shall not be infringed.

### Amendment III

No Soldier shall, in time of peace be quartered in any house, without the consent of the Owner, nor in time of war, but in a manner to be prescribed by law.

### Amendment IV

The right of the people to be secure in their persons, houses, papers, and effects, against unreasonable searches and seizures, shall not be violated, and no Warrants shall issue, but upon probable cause, supported by Oath or affirmation, and particularly describing the place to be searched, and the persons or things to be seized.

## Amendment V

No person shall be held to answer for a capital, or otherwise infamous crime, unless on a presentment or indictment of a Grand Jury, except in cases arising in the land or naval forces, or in the Militia, when in actual service in time of War or public danger; nor shall any person be subject for the same offence to be twice put in jeopardy of life or limb; nor shall be compelled in any criminal case to be a witness against himself, nor be deprived of life, liberty, or property, without due process of law; nor shall private property be taken for public use, without just compensation.

## Amendment VI

In all criminal prosecutions, the accused shall enjoy the right to a speedy and public trial, by an impartial jury of the State and district wherein the crime shall have been committed, which district shall have been previously ascertained by law, and to be informed of the nature and cause of the accusation; to be confronted with the witnesses against him; to have compulsory process for obtaining witnesses in his favor, and to have the Assistance of Counsel for his defence.

## Amendment VII

In Suits at common law, where the value in controversy shall exceed twenty dollars, the right of trial by jury shall be preserved, and no fact tried by a jury, shall be otherwise re-examined in any Court of the United States, than according to the rules of the common law.

## Amendment VIII

Excessive bail shall not be required, nor excessive fines imposed, nor cruel and unusual punishments inflicted.

## Amendment IX

The enumeration in the Constitution, of certain rights, shall not be construed to deny or disparage others retained by the people.

## Amendment X

The powers not delegated to the United States by the Constitution, nor prohibited by it to the States, are reserved to the States respectively, or to the people.
[First 10 amendments ratified 15 December 1791]

## Amendment XI

The Judicial power of the United States shall not be construed to extend to any suit in law or equity, commenced or prosecuted against one of the United States by Citizens of another State, or by Citizens or Subjects of any Foreign State.
[Ratified 7 February 1795]

## Amendment XII

The Electors shall meet in their respective states and vote by ballot for President and Vice-President, one of whom, at least, shall not be an inhabitant of the same state with themselves; they shall name in their ballots the person voted for as President, and in distinct ballots the person voted for as Vice-President, and they shall make distinct lists of all persons voted for as President, and of all persons voted for as Vice-President, and of the number of votes for each, which lists they shall sign and certify, and transmit sealed to the seat of the government of the United States, directed to the President of the Senate;—The President of the Senate shall, in the presence of the Senate and House of Representatives, open all the certificates and the votes shall then be counted;—The person having the greatest number of votes for President, shall be the President, if such number be a majority of the whole number of Electors appointed; and if no person have such majority, then from the persons having the highest numbers not exceeding three on the list of those voted for as President, the House of Representatives shall chuse immediately, by ballot, the President. But in chusing the President, the votes shall be taken by states, the representation from each state having one vote; a quorum for this purpose shall consist of a member or members from two-thirds of the states, and a majority of all the states shall be necessary to a choice. And if the House of Representatives shall not chuse a President whenever the right of choice shall devolve upon them, before the fourth day of March next following, then the Vice-President shall act as President, as in the case of the death or other constitutional disability of the President—The person having the greatest number of votes as Vice-President, shall be the Vice-President, if such number be a majority of the whole number of Electors

appointed, and if no person have a majority, then from the two highest numbers on the list, the Senate shall chuse the Vice-President; a quorum for the purpose shall consist of two-thirds of the whole number of Senators, and a majority of the whole number shall be necessary to a choice. But no person constitutionally ineligible to the office of President shall be eligible to that of Vice-President of the United States.
[Ratified 27 July 1804]

## Amendment XIII

*Section 1*. Neither slavery nor involuntary servitude, except as a punishment for crime whereof the party shall have been duly convicted, shall exist within the United States, or any place subject to their jurisdiction.

*Section 2*. Congress shall have power to enforce this article by appropriate legislation.
[Ratified 6 December 1865]

## Amendment XIV

*Section 1*. All persons born or naturalized in the United States and subject to the jurisdiction thereof, are citizens of the United States and of the State wherein they reside. No State shall make or enforce any law which shall abridge the privileges or immunities of citizens of the United States; nor shall any State deprive any person of life, liberty, or property, without due process of law; nor deny to any person within its jurisdiction the equal protection of the laws.

*Section 2*. Representatives shall be apportioned among the several States according to their respective numbers, counting the whole number of persons in each State, excluding Indians not taxed. But when the right to vote at any election for the choice of electors for President and Vice President of the United States, Representatives in Congress, the Executive and Judicial officers of a State, or the members of the Legislature thereof, is denied to any of the male inhabitants of such State, being twenty-one years of age, and citizens of the United States, or in any way abridged, except for participation in rebellion, or other crime, the basis of representation therein shall be reduced in the proportion which the number of such male citizens shall bear to the whole number of male citizens twenty-one years of age in such State.

*Section 3*. No person shall be a Senator or Representative in Congress, or elector of President and Vice President, or hold any office, civil or military, under the United States, or under any State, who, having previously taken an oath, as a member of Congress, or as an officer of the United States, or as a member of any State legislature, or as an executive or judicial officer of any State, to support the Constitution of the United States, shall have engaged in insurrection or rebellion against the same, or given aid or comfort to the enemies thereof. But Congress may by a vote of two-thirds of each House, remove such disability.

*Section 4.* The validity of the public debt of the United States, authorized by law, including debts incurred for payment of pensions and bounties for services in suppressing insurrection or rebellion, shall not be questioned. But neither the United States nor any State shall assume or pay any debt or obligation incurred in aid of insurrection or rebellion against the United States, or any claim for the loss or emancipation of any slave; but all such debts, obligations and claims shall be held illegal and void.

*Section 5.* The Congress shall have power to enforce, by appropriate legislation, the provisions of this article.
[Ratified 9 July 1868]

## Amendment XV

*Section 1.* The right of citizens of the United States to vote shall not be denied or abridged by the United States or by any State on account of race, color, or previous condition of servitude.

*Section 2.* The Congress shall have power to enforce this article by appropriate legislation.
[Ratified 3 February 1870]

## Amendment XVI

The Congress shall have power to lay and collect taxes on incomes, from whatever source derived, without apportionment among the several States, and without regard to any census or enumeration.
[Ratified 3 February 1913]

## Amendment XVII

The Senate of the United States shall be composed of two Senators from each State, elected by the people thereof, for six years; and each Senator shall have one vote. The electors in each State shall have the qualifications requisite for electors of the most numerous branch of the State legislatures.

When vacancies happen in the representation of any State in the Senate, the executive authority of such State shall issue writs of election to fill such vacancies: *Provided,* That the legislature of any State may empower the executive thereof to make temporary appointments until the people fill the vacancies by election as the legislature may direct.

This amendment shall not be so construed as to affect the election or term of any Senator chosen before it becomes valid as part of the Constitution. [Ratified 8 April 1913]

## Amendment XVIII

*Section 1.* After one year from the ratification of this article the manufacture, sale, or transportation of intoxicating liquors within, the importation thereof into, or the exportation thereof from the United States and all territory subject to the jurisdiction thereof for beverage purposes is hereby prohibited.

*Section 2.* The Congress and the several States shall have concurrent power to enforce this article by appropriate legislation.

*Section 3.* This article shall be inoperative unless it shall have been ratified as an amendment to the Constitution by the legislatures of the several States, as provided in the Constitution, within seven years from the date of the submission hereof to the States by the Congress. [Ratified 16 January 1919]

## Amendment XIX

The right of citizens of the United States to vote shall not be denied or abridged by the United States or by any State on account of sex.

Congress shall have power to enforce this article by appropriate legislation. [Ratified 18 August 1920]

## Amendment XX

*Section 1.* The terms of the President and Vice President shall end at noon on the 20th day of January, and the terms of Senators and Representatives at noon on the 3d day of January, of the years in which such terms would have ended if this article had not been ratified; and the terms of their successors shall then begin

*Section 2.* The Congress shall assemble at least once in every year, and such meeting shall begin at noon on the 3d day of January, unless they shall by law appoint a different day.

*Section 3.* If, at the time fixed for the beginning of the term of the President, the President elect shall have died, the Vice President elect shall become President. If a President shall not have been chosen before the time fixed for the beginning of his term, or if the President elect shall have failed to qualify, then the Vice President elect shall act as President until a President shall have qualified; and the Congress may by law provide for the case wherein neither a President elect nor a Vice President elect shall have qualified, declaring who shall then act as President, or the manner in which one who is to act shall be selected, and such person shall act accordingly until a President or Vice President shall have qualified.

*Section 4.* The Congress may by law provide for the case of the death of any of the persons from whom the House of Representatives may choose a President whenever the right of choice shall have devolved upon them, and for the case of the death of any of the persons from whom the Senate may choose a Vice President whenever the right of choice shall have devolved upon them.

*Section 5.* Sections 1 and 2 shall take effect on the 15th day of October following the ratification of this article.

*Section 6.* This article shall be inoperative unless it shall have been ratified as an amendment to the Constitution by the legislatures of three-fourths of the several States within seven years from the date of its submission.

[Ratified 23 January 1933]

## Amendment XXI

*Section 1.* The eighteenth article of amendment to the Constitution of the United States is hereby repealed.

*Section 2.* The transportation or importation into any State, Territory or possession of the United States for delivery or use therein of intoxicating liquors, in violation of the laws thereof, is hereby prohibited.

*Section 3.* This article shall be inoperative unless it shall have been ratified as an amendment to the Constitution by conventions in the several States, as provided in the Constitution, within seven years from the date of the submission hereof to the States by the Congress.

[Ratified 5 December 1933]

## Amendment XXII

*Section 1.* No person shall be elected to the office of the President more than twice, and no person who has held the office of President, or acted as President, for more than two years of a term to which some other person was elected President shall be elected to the office of the President more than once. But this article shall not apply to any person holding the office of President when this Article was proposed by the Congress, and shall not prevent any person who may be holding the office of President, or acting as President, during the term within which this Article become[s] operative from holding the office of President or acting as President during the remainder of such term.

Section 2. This Article shall be inoperative unless it shall have been ratified as an amendment to the Constitution by the legislatures of three-fourths of the several States within seven years from the date of its submission to the States by the Congress.

[Ratified 27 February 1951]

## Amendment XXIII

Section 1. The District constituting the seat of Government of the United States shall appoint in such manner as the Congress may direct:

A number of electors of President and Vice President equal to the whole number of Senators and Representatives in Congress to which the District would be entitled if it were a State, but in no event more than the least populous State; they shall be in addition to those appointed by the States, but they shall be considered, for the purposes of the election of President and Vice President, to be electors appointed by a State; and they shall meet in the District and perform such duties as provided by the twelfth article of amendment.

Section 2. The Congress shall have power to enforce this article by appropriate legislation.

[Ratified 29 March 1961]

## Amendment XXIV

Section 1. The right of citizens of the United States to vote in any primary or other election for President or Vice President, for electors for President or Vice President, or for Senator or Representative in Congress, shall not be denied or abridged by the United States or any State by reason of failure to pay any poll tax or other tax.

Section 2. The Congress shall have power to enforce this article by appropriate legislation.

[Ratified 23 January 1964]

## Amendment XXV

Section 1. In case of the removal of the President from office or of his death or resignation, the Vice President shall become President.

*Section 2.* Whenever there is a vacancy in the office of the Vice President, the President shall nominate a Vice President who shall take office upon confirmation by a majority vote of both Houses of Congress.

*Section 3.* Whenever the President transmits to the President pro tempore of the Senate and the Speaker of the House of Representatives his written declaration that he is unable to discharge the powers and duties of his office, and until he transmits to them a written declaration to the contrary, such powers and duties shall be discharged by the Vice President as Acting President.

*Section 4.* Whenever the Vice President and a majority of either the principal officers of the executive departments or of such other body as Congress may by law provide, transmit to the President pro tempore of the Senate and the Speaker of the House of Representatives their written declaration that the President is unable to discharge the powers and duties of his office, the Vice President shall immediately assume the powers and duties of the office as Acting President.

Thereafter, when the President transmits to the President pro tempore of the Senate and the Speaker of the House of Representatives his written declaration that no inability exists, he shall resume the powers and duties of his office unless the Vice President and a majority of either the principal officers of the executive department or of such other body as Congress may by law provide, transmit within four days to the President pro tempore of the Senate and the Speaker of the House of Representatives their written declaration that the President is unable to discharge the powers and duties of his office. Thereupon Congress shall decide the issue, assembling within forty-eight hours for that purpose if not in session. If the Congress, within twenty-one days after receipt of the latter written declaration, or, if Congress is not in session, within twenty-one days after Congress is required to assemble, determines by two-thirds vote of both houses that the President is unable to discharge the powers and duties of his office, the Vice President shall continue to discharge the same as Acting President; otherwise, the President shall resume the powers and duties of his office.
[Ratified 10 February 1967]

## Amendment XXVI

*Section 1.* The right of citizens of the United States, who are eighteen years of age or older, to vote shall not be denied or abridged by the United States or by any State on account of age.

*Section 2.* The Congress shall have power to enforce this article by appropriate legislation.
[Ratified 1 July 1971]

## Amendment XXVII

No law, varying the compensation for the services of the Senators and Representatives, shall take effect, until an election of Representatives shall have intervened.
[Ratified 7 May 1992]

# APPENDIX
# B

* * * * * * * * *

# Justices of the Supreme Court

| | Tenure | Appointed by | Replaced |
|---|---|---|---|
| JOHN JAY | 1789–1795 | Washington | |
| John Rutledge | 1789–1791 | Washington | |
| William Cushing | 1789–1810 | Washington | |
| James Wilson | 1789–1798 | Washington | |
| John Blair | 1789–1796 | Washington | |
| James Iredell | 1790–1799 | Washington | |
| Thomas Johnson | 1791–1793 | Washington | Rutledge |
| William Paterson | 1793–1806 | Washington | Johnson |
| JOHN RUTLEDGE | 1795 | Washington | Jay |
| Samuel Chase | 1796–1811 | Washington | Blair |
| OLIVER ELLSWORTH | 1796–1800 | Washington | Rutledge |
| Bushrod Washington | 1798–1829 | John Adams | Wilson |
| Alfred Moore | 1799–1804 | John Adams | Iredell |
| JOHN MARSHALL | 1801–1835 | John Adams | Ellsworth |
| William Johnson | 1804–1834 | Jefferson | Moore |
| Brockholst Livingston | 1806–1823 | Jefferson | Paterson |
| Thomas Todd | 1807–1826 | Jefferson | (new judgeship) |
| Gabriel Duval | 1811–1835 | Madison | Chase |

---

Chief justices' names appear in capital letters.

| | Tenure | Appointed by | Replaced |
|---|---|---|---|
| Joseph Story | 1811–1845 | Madison | Cushing |
| Smith Thompson | 1823–1843 | Monroe | Livingston |
| Robert Trimble | 1826–1828 | John Q. Adams | Todd |
| John McLean | 1829–1861 | Jackson | Trimble |
| Henry Baldwin | 1830–1844 | Jackson | Washington |
| James Wayne | 1835–1867 | Jackson | Johnson |
| ROGER B. TANEY | 1836–1864 | Jackson | Marshall |
| Phillip P. Barbour | 1836–1841 | Jackson | Duval |
| John Catron | 1837–1865 | Jackson | (new judgeship) |
| John McKinley | 1837–1852 | Van Buren | (new judgeship) |
| Peter V. Daniel | 1841–1860 | Van Buren | Barbour |
| Samuel Nelson | 1845–1872 | Tyler | Thompson |
| Levi Woodbury | 1845–1851 | Polk | Story |
| Robert C. Grier | 1846–1870 | Polk | Baldwin |
| Benjamin R. Curtis | 1851–1857 | Fillmore | Woodbury |
| John A. Campbell | 1853–1861 | Pierce | McKinley |
| Nathan Clifford | 1858–1881 | Buchanan | Curtis |
| Noah H. Swayne | 1862–1881 | Lincoln | McLean |
| Samuel F. Miller | 1862–1890 | Lincoln | Daniel |
| David Davis | 1862–1877 | Lincoln | Campbell |
| Stephen J. Field | 1863–1897 | Lincoln | (new judgeship) |
| SALMON CHASE | 1864–1873 | Lincoln | Taney |
| William Strong | 1870–1880 | Grant | Grier |
| Joseph P. Bradley | 1870–1892 | Grant | Wayne |
| Ward Hunt | 1872–1882 | Grant | Nelson |
| MORRISON R. WAITE | 1874–1888 | Grant | Chase |
| John Marshall Harlan | 1877–1911 | Hayes | Davis |
| William B. Woods | 1880–1887 | Hayes | Strong |
| Stanley Matthews | 1881–1889 | Garfield | Swayne |
| Horace Gray | 1881–1902 | Arthur | Clifford |
| Samuel Blatchford | 1881–1893 | Arthur | Hunt |
| Lucius Q. C. Lamar | 1888–1893 | Cleveland | Woods |
| MELVILLE W. FULLER | 1888–1910 | Cleveland | Waite |
| David J. Brewer | 1889–1910 | Harrison | Matthews |

| | Tenure | Appointed by | Replaced |
|---|---|---|---|
| Henry B. Brown | 1890–1906 | Harrison | Miller |
| George Shiras, Jr. | 1892–1903 | Harrison | Bradley |
| Howell E. Jackson | 1893–1895 | Harrison | Lamar |
| Edward D. White | 1894–1910 | Cleveland | Blatchford |
| Rufus W. Peckham | 1895–1909 | Cleveland | Jackson |
| Joseph McKenna | 1898–1925 | McKinley | Field |
| Oliver Wendell Holmes | 1902–1932 | T. Roosevelt | Gray |
| William R. Day | 1903–1922 | T. Roosevelt | Shiras |
| William H. Moody | 1906–1910 | T. Roosevelt | Brown |
| Horace H. Lurton | 1909–1914 | Taft | Peckham |
| Charles Evans Hughes | 1910–1916 | Taft | Brewer |
| EDWARD D. WHITE | 1910–1921 | Taft | Fuller |
| Willis Van Devanter | 1910–1937 | Taft | White |
| Joseph R. Lamar | 1910–1916 | Taft | Moody |
| Mahlon Pitney | 1912–1922 | Taft | Harlan |
| James McReynolds | 1914–1941 | Wilson | Lurton |
| Louis D. Brandeis | 1916–1939 | Wilson | Lamar |
| John H. Clarke | 1916–1922 | Wilson | Hughes |
| WILLIAM H. TAFT | 1921–1930 | Harding | White |
| George Sutherland | 1922–1938 | Harding | Clarke |
| Pierce Butler | 1922–1939 | Harding | Day |
| Edward T. Sanford | 1923–1930 | Harding | Pitney |
| Harlan F. Stone | 1925–1941 | Coolidge | McKenna |
| CHARLES EVANS HUGHES | 1930–1941 | Hoover | Taft |
| Owen J. Roberts | 1930–1945 | Hoover | Sanford |
| Benjamin N. Cardozo | 1932–1938 | Hoover | Holmes |
| Hugo L. Black | 1937–1971 | F. Roosevelt | Van Devanter |
| Stanley F. Reed | 1938–1957 | F. Roosevelt | Sutherland |
| Felix Frankfurter | 1939–1962 | F. Roosevelt | Cardozo |
| William O. Douglas | 1939–1975 | F. Roosevelt | Brandeis |
| Frank Murphy | 1940–1949 | F. Roosevelt | Butler |
| James F. Byrnes | 1941–1942 | F. Roosevelt | McReynolds |

| | Tenure | Appointed by | Replaced |
|---|---|---|---|
| HARLAN F. STONE | 1941–1946 | F. Roosevelt | Hughes |
| Robert H. Jackson | 1941–1954 | F. Roosevelt | Stone |
| Wiley B. Rutledge | 1943–1949 | F. Roosevelt | Byrnes |
| Harold H. Burton | 1945–1958 | Truman | Roberts |
| FRED M. VINSON | 1946–1953 | Truman | Stone |
| Tom C. Clark | 1949–1967 | Truman | Murphy |
| Sherman Minton | 1949–1956 | Truman | Rutledge |
| EARL WARREN | 1953–1969 | Eisenhower | Vinson |
| John M. Harlan | 1955–1971 | Eisenhower | Jackson |
| William J. Brennan | 1956–1990 | Eisenhower | Minton |
| Charles E. Whittaker | 1957–1962 | Eisenhower | Reed |
| Potter Stewart | 1958–1981 | Eisenhower | Burton |
| Byron R. White | 1962–1993 | Kennedy | Whittaker |
| Arthur J. Goldberg | 1962–1965 | Kennedy | Frankfurter |
| Abe Fortas | 1965–1969 | Johnson | Goldberg |
| Thurgood Marshall | 1967–1991 | Johnson | Clark |
| WARREN E. BURGER | 1969–1986 | Nixon | Warren |
| Harry A. Blackmun | 1970–1994 | Nixon | Fortas |
| Lewis F. Powell | 1971–1987 | Nixon | Black |
| William H. Rehnquist | 1971– | Nixon | Harlan |
| John Paul Stevens | 1975– | Ford | Douglas |
| Sandra Day O'Connor | 1981– | Reagan | Stewart |
| WILLIAM H. REHNQUIST | 1986– | Reagan | Burger |
| Antonin Scalia | 1986– | Reagan | Rehnquist |
| Anthony M. Kennedy | 1988– | Reagan | Powell |
| David H. Souter | 1990– | Bush | Brennan |
| Clarence Thomas | 1991– | Bush | Marshall |
| Ruth Bader Ginsburg | 1993– | Clinton | White |
| Stephen Breyer | 1994– | Clinton | Blackmun |

# INDEX

❋ ❋ ❋ ❋ ❋ ❋ ❋ ❋ ❋

## by Virgil Diodato